# Hardwick
## a great house
## and its estate

# An England's Past for Everyone paperback

# Hardwick

## a great house and its estate

PHILIP RIDEN
AND
DUDLEY FOWKES

Phillimore

First published 2009

A Victoria County History publication
Published by Phillimore & Co. Ltd, Madam Green Farm Business Centre,
Oving, Chichester, West Sussex, England in association with the Institute of
Historical Research at the University of London.
www.phillimore.co.uk

ISBN 978-1-86077-544-4

British Library Cataloguing in Publication Data. A cataloguing record for this
book is available from the British Library.

Typeset in Humanist 521 and Minion


We wish particularly to thank the following EPE and VCH staff for their efforts
during the production of this volume:

John Beckett – Director of the Victoria County History
Matthew Bristow – Historic Environment Research Manager
Sarah Byrne – Production Assistant
Catherine Cavanagh – Project Manager
Jessica Davies – Publications Manager
Skye Dillon – Education and Skills Manager
Nafisa Gaffar – Finance and Contracts Officer
Mel Hackett – Communications Manager
Nick Hall – Administrator
Dmitri Nemchenko – Web Manager
Alan Thacker – Executive Editor of the Victoria County History
Elizabeth Williamson – Architectural Editor of the Victoria County History


Printed and bound in Malta.

Front Cover: Aerial view of Hardwick Old and New Halls (courtesy of English
    Heritage Photo Library).
Back Cover: Bess of Hardwick as a young woman (courtesy of National Trust
    Picture Library/Angela Hornak).

# Contents

# Foreword

I have always regarded Bess of Hardwick as the spiritual inspiration of the Cavendish dynasty which she founded. Until this book appeared I had also believed that she was, with her husband William Cavendish, responsible for the landed estates especially around Chatsworth which have remained the core landholding of my family ever since. Philip Riden's work, however, revises that traditional view and suggests that this achievement was only partly to Bess's credit and that more weight should be given to her brother James as well as her second son and eventual principal heir, William, the first Earl of Devonshire.

For all the hundreds and thousands of people who admire Hardwick as one of Britain's most beautiful architectural triumphs this book will be essential reading. It describes much of the background to the way in which Bess's estates were administered and what life was like at Hardwick, Bess's principal home and very close to where she was born, built on land that had been farmed by her father and no doubt his father before him.

For today's visitors to Chatsworth this book will also explain how it is only in the last 50 years, since my parents came to live here, that Chatsworth has been our family's main and most occupied house. Before then Hardwick was much favoured by many of my ancestors, most recently by my great-grandmother, Duchess Evelyn, who spent over 20 years living there after the death of her husband, the 9th duke, in 1938.

A further part in the history of Hardwick which will be of great interest to all local people is the recent history of the district around the house, especially since Hardwick Hall and its park were transferred to the National Trust to help pay our family's death duties in the late 1950s. This history is dominated by two themes: the decline of the coal industry and the mining villages that served it, and the evolution of the farming villages in the area, now mainly occupied by people who no longer work on the land.

All in all this is an utterly compelling book which fills several important gaps in the history both of Hardwick and of Chatsworth.

*Devonshire*

*The Duke of Devonshire, KCVO, CBE, DL*
*2009*

# Preface

This is the second of two paperbacks about places in north-east Derbyshire prepared as part of the England's Past for Everyone project funded by an award to the University of London by the Heritage Lottery Fund to enable the Victoria County History to widen the scope of its work. The first, on *Bolsover: Castle, Town and Colliery*, was published in 2008. As with the earlier title, additional material not included in the book can be found on an associated website (www.ExploreEnglandsPast.org.uk).

The award from the HLF has been augmented by funds raised by the Derbyshire VCH Trust and by help from Derbyshire County Council and the University of Nottingham, which has administered the Derbyshire portion of the HLF award.

Some of the research incorporated in this book has been done by groups of volunteers meeting under our leadership at Doe Lea and Chesterfield Local Studies Library; in particular we would like to thank Cecil Hill of Tibshelf for sharing with us his knowledge of farming around Hardwick, and Pat Mellor, who also knows the area well and did the bulk of the analysis of census enumerators' books included in chapter 6. We are equally grateful to Richard Sheppard of Trent and Peak Archaeology for his specialist report on farm buildings in Ault Hucknall parish, the results of which are similarly incorporated in chapter 6.

Our greatest debt is to the Duke of Devonshire, KCVO, CBE, DL, for allowing the fullest possible access to his very extensive muniments relating to the Hardwick estate, which his ancestors owned from the early 13th century until 1959, now preserved at Chatsworth. The richness of this source, and the extent to which we have been able to make use of it over a long period, have enabled us, within the limits of a short study aimed at a general readership, to give a much fuller picture than has previously been available of both the growth of the estate in the 16th century and its subsequent management. We are extremely grateful not only to the Duke but also to Mr Matthew Hirst, the Director of Arts and Historic Collections at Chatsworth, and his staff for their enthusiastic support.

Other research has been done at the local studies libraries at Chesterfield and Matlock, the Derbyshire Record Office, Lichfield Record Office and Mansfield local studies library, to all of whom we are indebted for the facilities provided. We are also grateful to other institutions which have provided some of the illustrations reproduced here, to the EPE team in London and to an external referee for comments on the text.

Philip Riden
Dudley Fowkes

## HARDWICK'S OWNERS

**1546**
James Hardwick comes of age and succeeds to the family estate.

**1579**
James Hardwick's estates pass into receivership.

**1583**
William Cavendish, Bess's second son, buys Hardwick and James's other estates.

**1590**
Bess is widowed for the last time and William's transfers Hardwick to his mother.

**1608**
Bess dies and her purchased lands pass to her son William, now Lord Cavendish.

**1618**
Lord Cavendish is created earl of Devonshire earl of Devonshire.

**1626-8**
The 1st earl of Devonshire dies and is briefly succeeded by his son William.

**1638**
The 3rd earl of Devonshire comes of age and enters into the family's estate.

**1684-94**
The 3rd earl dies and is succeeded by son who, ten years later, is promoted to become duke of Devonshire.

**1700**
Hardwick ceases to be the administrative centre of the Cavendish estates.

**1811**
The 6th duke inherits and takes more interest in Hardwick than his predecessors.

**1868**
The 7th duke gives his eldest son, the marquess of Hartington, a life interest in the Hardwick estate.

**1938**
The 9th duke dies, leaving Hardwick to his widow Duchess Evelyn as a dower house.

**1950**
The 10th duke dies prematurely, exposing the estate to very heavy death duties.

**1959**
The two mansions and park at Hardwick are transferred to HM Treasury.

**1960**
The National Trust opens Hardwick Hall to the public and also acquires the park.

## 1500

## 1600

## 1700

## 1800

## 1900

## MAIN EVENTS

**c.1546-72**
James Hardwick enlarges the family's estate.

**1567**
Bess marries her fourth husband George Talbot earl of Shrewsbury.

**1583**
Bess separates from her husband and moves to Hardwick, bought for her by her son.

**1587-91**
Bess greatly extends the Old Hall at Hardwick.

**1591-8**
Bess builds a new mansion alongside the Old Hall, which remains occupied.

**1609-26**
William Senior undertakes a survey of the Cavendish estate for the 1st earl.

**1612**
The 'New Inn' is built and becomes the administrative headquarters of the family's estates north of the Trent.

**1616**
The 1st earl of Devonshire buys Chatsworth from his brother Henry.

**1626**
A magnificent monument to the 1st earl and Henry Cavendish is erected at Edensor.

**1642-5**
The 3rd earl goes into exile during the Civil War.

**1688-94**
The 4th earl rebuilds the mansion at Chatsworth.

**1745-67**
The Old Hall at Hardwick is partly demolished.

**1785-91**
The 5th duke carries out some modernisation at the New Hall.

**1840-58**
The 6th duke greatly improves both the Hall and estate at Hardwick.

**1868-91**
The marquess of Hartington develops Hardwick as a sporting estate.

**1870s**
The beginning of large-scale coal mining in the parishes around Hardwick.

**1938-60**
Duchess Evelyn, the widow of the 9th duke, makes Hardwick her home.

**1965**
The M1 is opened through Derbyshire, skirting Hardwick to the west.

**1968-70**
Hardwick and Williamthorpe collieries close.

# Hardwick and its Owners

*Figure 1* Timeline showing changes of ownership of the Hardwick estate and main events in its history.

Hardwick Hall, which stands prominently on high ground overlooking the valley of the river Doe Lea in north-east Derbyshire, about six miles from Chesterfield, is among the most magnificent great houses of the Elizabethan period. Equally, its builder, Elizabeth dowager countess of Shrewsbury (*c.*1521-1608), best known to history as 'Bess of Hardwick', is probably the third most famous Englishwoman of her age after Queen Elizabeth herself and Mary Queen of Scots, with both of whom Bess had close links. The hall itself, built in the 1590s, is one of the most important, as well as one of the best preserved, projects undertaken by Robert Smythson, the leading designer of great houses of the late 16th century.

Much has been written on the architectural history of Hardwick Hall, and on its contents; even more has been written about Bess of Hardwick. This book is not another history of Hardwick, nor an addition to the long list of biographies of its builder. Instead it is an attempt to look at the wider history of the estate of which Hardwick was the centre, before, during and after Bess's lifetime. Despite its later importance, Hardwick was not a medieval manor: it was a freehold tenement established in the early 13th century within the manor of Stainsby, which originally occupied the whole of the adjoining parishes of Ault Hucknall and Heath. Until the mid-16th century the Hardwick family's estate barely extended beyond Ault Hucknall parish and throughout the Middle Ages the Hardwick family, although long established, were minor landowners whose horizons were limited to the Scarsdale district of north-east Derbyshire, rather than to the county as a whole.

It was Bess's younger brother James Hardwick (1525-*c.*1580) who greatly enlarged his family's estate through a series of purchases in both Derbyshire and Nottinghamshire. James overreached himself and died heavily in debt. In 1583 Bess's second son William (one of six children she had with her second husband, also named William Cavendish, who died in 1557), bought James Hardwick's estate for his mother. Bess was then married to her fourth husband, George Talbot, 6th earl of Shrewsbury, and thus unable to hold property in her own name. Despite this, during the 1580s, Bess began building a new and much grander house at Hardwick, the Old Hall, as it is known today to distinguish it from the mansion of the 1590s. The Hardwick estate was the largest of a number of purchases made

Elizabeth Countess of Shrewsbury.
*The Original in the Cavendish Family.*

*Figure 2* Elizabeth Talbot, countess of Shrewsbury, better known as Bess of Hardwick, with her signature and seal.

by William and his younger brother Charles Cavendish during their mother's fourth marriage. These gave all three an income independent of whatever might be provided by Shrewsbury, from whom Bess was estranged for most of the 1580s.

After Shrewsbury died in 1590 Bess was able to claim her widow's dower income of around £3,000 a year from his son and heir, Gilbert Talbot, the 7th earl. This, together with the income from her other estates, provided her with sufficient means to build Hardwick Hall and a second house nearby at Oldcotes, intended as a home for her son William. At the same time William, by now regarded by his mother as her *de facto* heir, continued to enlarge his own estate, mainly in

*Figure 3*  William Cavendish, 1st earl of Devonshire (1551-1626), towards the end of his life. An impressive portrait of an impressive man, the epitome of the successful Jacobean magnate.

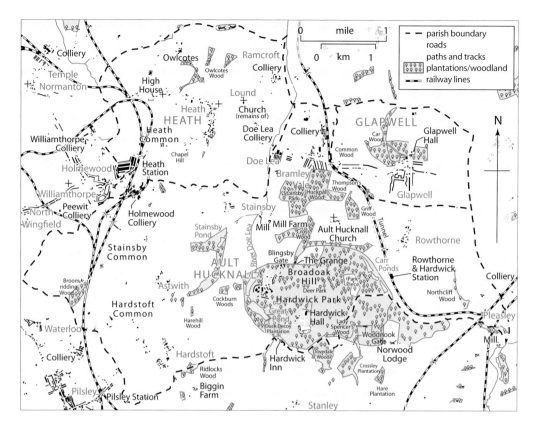

*Figure 4* Map of the Hardwick estate, showing the places discussed in this book. Parish names are in capitals.

*Figure 5* Derbyshire in the English Midlands.

Derbyshire, while his brother Charles established himself in Nottinghamshire in a house at Welbeck. Charles also bought the manor of Bolsover, where he began building a new mansion on the site of the medieval castle. Both these estates were purchased from Gilbert Talbot, who was Charles's step-brother and brother-in-law.

William Cavendish's position was greatly enhanced when his mother died in 1608, leaving him all the lands she had bought in her last widowhood. Meanwhile, the estate created in the early 1550s by her second husband, Sir William Cavendish, centred on Chatsworth in the Peak, passed to her eldest son Henry. He had settled at Tutbury, just over the border in Staffordshire, after marrying Gilbert Talbot's sister Grace. Henry appears to have been a poor manager of his lands and, shortly after their mother died, accepted an offer from his brother, William, whereby William paid him an immediate cash sum (and a pension to Grace if she outlived her husband) in return for acquiring most of Henry's estates at his death. Thus in 1616 William Cavendish, by then Lord Cavendish of Hardwick, united the Hardwick estate, originally created by James Hardwick and augmented by Bess, with both the Chatsworth estate and his own acquisitions over the previous 20 years. He at once became the largest landowner in Derbyshire and, when he was created earl of Devonshire two years later, one of the wealthiest members of the Jacobean peerage.

As soon as he inherited his mother's estates, Cavendish commissioned a detailed survey of all his lands, beginning with those around Hardwick. The maps and accompanying written descriptions ('terriers') produced in 1609-10 provide both a good picture of the estate at that date and also clues as to the earlier appearance of the landscape. All the villages on the Hardwick estate (Heath, Stainsby, Astwith, Hardstoft and Rowthorne, and the deserted village of Lound, which lay about half a mile east of Heath) cultivated their land in the Middle Ages in either three or four open fields. Parts of these fields remained in use in the early 17th century, although some land had been fenced off and divided into small fields which contemporaries called 'closes'. Slightly further afield, Langwith and Stony Houghton each had their own open fields. The existence of open-field cultivation in north-east Derbyshire is sometimes difficult to appreciate because in most places the system disappeared long before Parliamentary enclosure in the 18th century. Only for a few parishes are there either earlier maps or traces of 'ridge and furrow' on the ground today to identify land that once lay within a medieval open field.

One place where such earthworks can be seen is in Hardwick park, to the south and west of the Hall. This shows that the creation of the park, which seems to have been begun by James Hardwick and enlarged by Bess before being extended again in the 17th century, involved taking arable land out of cultivation. There is no evidence for a park at Hardwick in the Middle Ages, although there was one around the manor house at Stainsby, most of which had been converted to farmland by the early 17th century. There was also a large park at Langwith, parts of which survive today as woodland. Other land in the parishes around Hardwick remained unenclosed common waste until the era of Parliamentary enclosure. These commons included some 300 acres on either side of the road from Temple Normanton to Tibshelf, which belonged to the manor of Stainsby and was not enclosed until 1832, and about a thousand acres lying midway between Langwith, Pleasley and Stony Houghton, enclosed under an Act of 1748.

The 1st earl of Devonshire died in 1626 aged seventy-four. His son outlived him by barely two years, dying young and heavily in debt. During the 1630s his widow, Countess Christian, restored the

*Figure 6* View from the south-west of part of the Hardwick estate, showing the two Halls and service buildings on the edge of a steep escarpment, with a plateau stretching to the north and rolling countryside beyond.

family's financial position and handed the estate over to her son William, the 3rd earl, when he came of age in 1638. Although his younger brother, Charles Cavendish, fought and died in the king's service during the Civil War and his mother was a minor Royalist figure in the 1650s, the 3rd earl concentrated on keeping his estate intact during the troubles of the mid-17th century. In this he was generally successful, although there were few additions to the estate during his lifetime and his income was stable, rather than rising, even after the Restoration. The earl divided his time between London and the country, and when in Derbyshire lived both at Chatsworth, at the house built by Bess in the 1550s and 1560s, and at Hardwick, the administrative centre of the estate in the county. He died in 1684.

The 4th earl was created duke of Devonshire in 1694 as a reward for his part in the Glorious Revolution of 1688. He made no major additions to his family's estate. In 1700, after completing the rebuilding of the mansion at Chatsworth to create the core of the building visitors see today, he also reorganised how the estate was run. From this date administration was concentrated in London, and the Derbyshire portion was managed from Chatsworth. Throughout the 18th century Hardwick Hall remained furnished

*Figure 7* Heath Road, Holmewood, part of the village built for miners at the nearby colliery, photographed in the 1920s or 1930s.

and was occasionally occupied by the family, although the Old Hall was allowed to become ruinous. In the early 19th century the 6th duke spent more time at Hardwick than his immediate predecessors, and in the 1840s and 1850s he modernised the Hall and improved the farms on the estate. In the second half of the 19th century Hardwick became the home of the future 8th duke, the Liberal Unionist MP who sat in the Commons as marquess of Hartington, although when he succeeded to the dukedom in 1891 he made Chatsworth his principal country residence. The last member of the family to live at Hardwick was the widow of the 9th duke, Duchess Evelyn, for whom it served as a dower house until her death in 1960. The year before Duchess Evelyn died the Hall and park were transferred by the trustees of the 11th duke to HM Treasury (which in turn conveyed them to the National Trust) in partial settlement of the death duties payable following the death of the 10th duke in 1950.

Apart from minor disposals by the widow of the 2nd earl, some small acquisitions by the 3rd earl, and the purchase in the 1940s of Lord Bathurst's property at Scarcliffe and that of the duke of Portland around Bolsover, the Hardwick estate was much the same size and shape in 1959 as it had been in 1626. Its contribution to the family's total income diminished in the 18th and early 19th centuries, notably following their inheritance of the Burlington estates as a a result of the future 4th duke's marriage in 1748. The Hardwick estate remained agricultural throughout most of the period covered by this book, but in the late 19th century income from coal royalties gradually overtook the farm rental as large-scale mining developed. As a result, in common with the Staveley and Chesterfield estates to the north and the smaller Blackwell property to the south, both of which also lay on coal-bearing land, the Hardwick estate grew in relative importance during this period.

The expansion of coal mining transformed the character of the district around Hardwick and the landscape of the area, as well as blackening the walls of the Hall. Small-scale mining had taken place on the estate since Bess's day, mainly it seems to supply the Hall rather than for outside sale, but it was only after the Top Hard seam began to be exploited after 1870 that large collieries were opened near Hardwick. They were served by new railways and accompanied by new housing for the miners. Like most landowners, the Cavendishes kept collieries out of the park and out of sight of the mansion, but the pits at Glapwell, Holmewood, Williamthorpe, Tibshelf and Pleasley were all within a couple of miles of Hardwick. Langwith colliery was close to the village of Upper Langwith. The older pattern of settlement in Ault Hucknall

*Figure 8* The impact of the railways on the Hardwick area. As the network expanded, so did the number of collieries and the new villages built to house miners. Parish names are in capitals and settlements in orange.

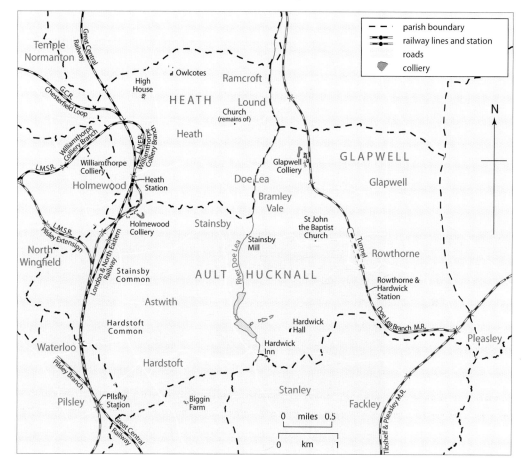

and the other parishes near Hardwick was overlain by new colliery villages at places like Doe Lea, Holmewood, New Houghton and Whaley Thorns. The population of the district grew more rapidly than in the past and its character changed, as mining families came to live close to (although not usually alongside) farmers and farm labourers. This created, in the parishes around Hardwick, a society not unlike that portrayed in the novels of D.H. Lawrence for an area slightly to the south. Landowners in the coalfield welcomed the income from royalties but at the same time they and their tenants had to put up with increased poaching and damage, the dirt and grime inseparable from large-scale coalmining and, especially after 1918, a challenge to their traditional authority in local government.

This mixed society began to break up at much the same time as the National Trust took over Hardwick and opened it to the public. The Hall had not previously been open to visitors, although local people had been free to walk in the park. The opening of the M1 motorway through east Derbyshire in 1965 made the house more visible and more accessible to people from a wider area. At the same time, the Chatsworth estate began to sell off cottages and redundant farmhouses and farm buildings in the villages around Hardwick to incomers who wanted to live in the country but be close to the motorway network. The collieries also began to close in the 1960s. With little alternative employment, villages like Holmewood, Doe Lea and Bramley Vale became deeply depressed. The sharp contrast between the two communities that had always existed remained but changed in character: as new wealth came into the old farming villages the fragile prosperity provided for a time by mining drained away from the pit villages. Despite the best efforts of the local authorities to improve housing, schools and other facilities, as well

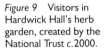

*Figure 9*    Visitors in Hardwick Hall's herb garden, created by the National Trust *c.* 2000.

as introducing new employment, this gulf remains to the present day. Nor has the emergence of Hardwick as a major destination for day visitors helped the wider community. Most visitors (other than local residents) either come over to Hardwick as part of a short break in the more congenial surroundings of the Peak District, or arrive for the day by motorway from almost anywhere in England. They do not stay and spend money locally, except perhaps to have lunch at the *Hardwick Inn*.

The following chapters discuss in more detail the aspects of the history of Hardwick mentioned briefly here: the growth of the estate at the hands of James Hardwick in the mid-16th century; the absorption of Hardwick into a larger unit in 1583 and the building of not one but two new mansions on the site of an older house; Hardwick's importance as the administrative hub of the estate in the 17th century and its relative decline in the 18th century; its revival in the 19th century and the changes wrought by the growth of coal mining; and the further changes of the 20th century following the break-up of the estate and the decline of mining.

# Chapter 2

# The Making of a Great Estate

The transformation of Hardwick in the 16th century from the home of a minor gentry family, whose lands were largely confined to the parish in which they lived, into the centre of the largest estate in Derbyshire is a story that has been told on several occasions, usually as the central theme in the life of Bess of Hardwick. Accounts of her modest birth, her four marriages to ever wealthier husbands, and her ruthless aggrandisement of her family at the expense of all who stood in her way, symbolised by her building projects at Chatsworth and Hardwick, go back to the late 17th century, to within a couple of generations of her death in 1608. Clearly, if only because of her longevity (she was about eighty-six when she died), Bess is an important figure in the story related in this chapter, but to concentrate entirely on her life and work is to misunderstand the process by which the estate centred on Hardwick grew so dramatically. The contributions made by three others, her brother James Hardwick, her second husband Sir William Cavendish, and her second son William Cavendish, 1st earl of Devonshire, need to be taken into account, as do the simple accidents of birth, marriage and death, not to mention sheer good luck. This chapter examines the complex sequence of events that began with the coming of age in 1546 of James Hardwick and ended with the death of his nephew, the 1st earl of Devonshire, 80 years later.[1]

## JAMES HARDWICK

When Bess and James's grandfather, John Hardwick, died in 1507 his estate was described, in the formulaic usage of the inquisitions held by the Chancery following the death of landowners, as comprising six messuages, 200 acres of arable land, 20 acres of meadow and 30 acres of pasture in the lordship of Stainsby, together with half a bovate of land in Glapwell, held of John Leeke's manor of Pleasley. Taken literally, this suggests that the main portion of the estate consisted of a chief residence (Hardwick Hall) and five tenanted farms; some of the land would presumably have been farmed by the family themselves and the rest let to tenants. There was certainly a home farm at Hardwick in Bess's day and for a long time afterwards.[2]

John's son and heir, also named John, was only 12 when his
father died, and so the estate would have remained in the hands of
his widowed mother Elizabeth until he came of age. The younger
John was already married, or at least espoused, at the time of his
father's death, to Elizabeth, the daughter of Thomas Leeke of
Hasland. The couple would not have lived as man and wife for
some years after 1507, probably not until John turned 21 in 1516
and would have taken possession of his estates. He and Elizabeth
had six surviving children, a son and five daughters, all born before
1528, when John died in his early thirties, leaving his widow to deal
with her husband's executors. They had been given instructions to
pay her sufficient from his estate to bring up the children. She also
had to try to find husbands for her daughters with little to offer in
the way of a dowry.

Elizabeth remarried the year after John died, to Ralph Leche
of Chatsworth, a younger son of another local gentry family of
probably about the same standing as the Hardwicks and the branch
of the Leekes to which she belonged. Elizabeth had three more
daughters with Ralph, although the marriage was blighted by his
financial problems and an allegation that he deserted his wife.
Leche spent part of the 1540s imprisoned for debt in London. By
the time James Hardwick came of age in 1546 one of his sisters
(Dorothy) had died, another (Bess) had been briefly married and
widowed almost straightaway, and the husband of a third, Godfrey
Boswell of Penistone in south Yorkshire, was complaining that her
father's executors were refusing to hand over the portion from his
estate to which his wife was entitled.

James Hardwick's own career is not as well documented as
Bess's, but it appears that, despite the modest circumstances of
his own upbringing, he was determined to expand the estate
he had inherited from his father. The 1550s and 1560s were in
principle a good time to do this, since land that had previously
been owned by either the religious houses dissolved in the 1530s
or the gilds and chantries abolished in 1548 was coming onto
the market. Almost all the counties of England provide examples
of families who acquired wealth in this period through the
purchase of former monastic estates. James was not one of the
major figures in this process in Derbyshire, in the way in which
both the 5th and 6th earls of Shrewsbury were, as the heads of
the most important magnate family in the region. Nor does he
rank alongside the heads of leading county gentry families with
seats in Scarsdale such as the Foljambes of Walton or the Leekes
of Sutton. James would not have had the resources to compete
with families like these, simply because his existing estates would
not have generated sufficient income to provide surplus funds

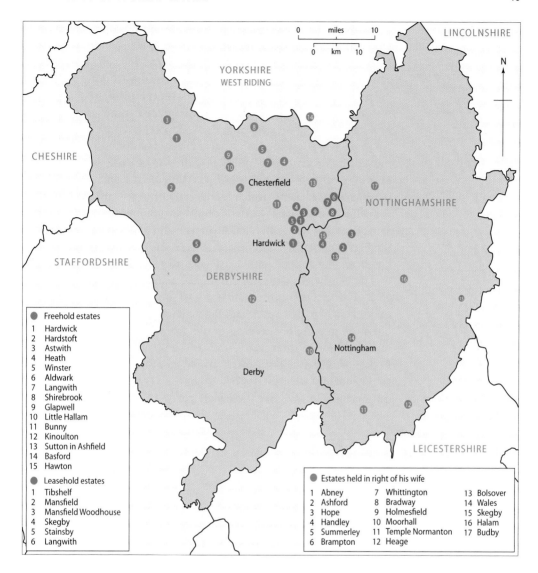

0    miles    10

0    km    10

LINCOLNSHIRE

YORKSHIRE
WEST RIDING

N

CHESHIRE

Chesterfield

NOTTINGHAMSHIRE

STAFFORDSHIRE

Hardwick

DERBYSHIRE

Nottingham

Derby

LEICESTERSHIRE

● Freehold estates
1   Hardwick
2   Hardstoft
3   Astwith
4   Heath
5   Winster
6   Aldwark
7   Langwith
8   Shirebrook
9   Glapwell
10  Little Hallam
11  Bunny
12  Kinoulton
13  Sutton in Ashfield
14  Basford
15  Hawton

● Leasehold estates
1   Tibshelf
2   Mansfield
3   Mansfield Woodhouse
4   Skegby
5   Stainsby
6   Langwith

● Estates held in right of his wife

| 1 | Abney | 7 | Whittington | 13 | Bolsover |
| 2 | Ashford | 8 | Bradway | 14 | Wales |
| 3 | Hope | 9 | Holmesfield | 15 | Skegby |
| 4 | Handley | 10 | Moorhall | 16 | Halam |
| 5 | Summerley | 11 | Temple Normanton | 17 | Budby |
| 6 | Brampton | 12 | Heage | | |

*Figure 11*  Map of James
Hardwick's estates
in 1570.

to buy other lands. In fact, James borrowed to buy land, and at
the end of his life he was hopelessly in debt, mainly it seems to
London merchants.

James Hardwick was clearly a man in a hurry but he was not
one of the new rich of his generation, in the way in which his
much more successful brother-in-law Sir William Cavendish was.
When the heralds visited Derbyshire for the first time in 1569
to verify claims by landowning families to their coats of arms,
James Hardwick produced a pedigree going back five generations
to a William Hardwick who lived in the early 15th century. By
piecing together references to earlier members of the family
in family muniments and legal records, it is in fact possible to

*Figures 12 (below) and 13 (right)* Chart pedigrees of the descendants of Jocelin of Stainsby and of the Hardwick family from *c*.1400 to Bess's day. The estates descended through those named in red.

trace a reasonably robust pedigree for the family from the early 13th century, when they first arrived in Derbyshire.

James was allowed both arms and crest in 1569. The arms consisted of a silver shield with a blue saltire cross. Along the top of the shield there was another band of blue, on which were three five-leaf devices in silver. The crest was equally grand, consisting of a stag standing on a mound, dressed in gold, with a collar of red and silver roses round his neck. Given the modest position of most of James's medieval ancestors, and the lack of any surviving examples of these arms on seals, it is difficult to be certain that his family had used arms (much less a crest) from an early date. On the other hand, James Hardwick himself did not obtain a grant of arms (as other newly rich landowners of his generation did) and the heralds evidently accepted that the arms they noted in 1569 had been in use since for at least a century and a half.[3]

The Hardwicks were not among the leading figures of 15th-century Derbyshire. The heads of the family did not hold major office in the county and their marriage partners (none of whom were heiresses) were drawn from families in much the same position as themselves, such as the Barleys of Barlow or the Leekes of Hasland. Nor is there any sign of the Hardwicks adding significantly to their estates by purchase rather than marriage in this period. Families like these were parish gentry, not county

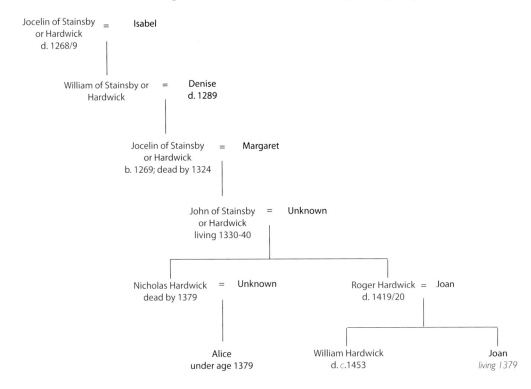

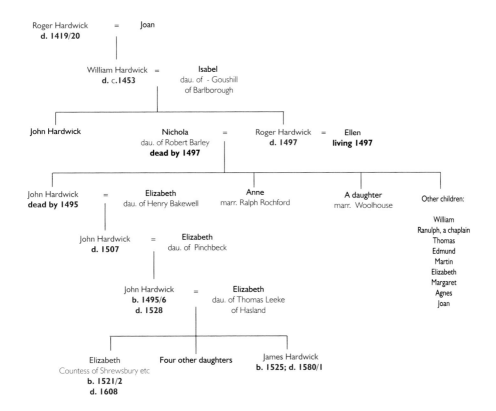

Roger Hardwick = Joan
d. 1419/20

William Hardwick = Isabel
d. c.1453          dau. of - Goushill
                   of Barlborough

John Hardwick        Nichola        =    Roger Hardwick    =    Ellen
                dau. of Robert Barley         d. 1497          living 1497
                   dead by 1497

John Hardwick    =    Elizabeth         Anne              A daughter        Other children:
dead by 1495      dau. of Henry Bakewell  marr. Ralph Rochford   marr. Woolhouse
                                                                            William
                                                                            Ranulph, a chaplain
John Hardwick    =    Elizabeth                                             Thomas
d. 1507           dau. of Pinchbeck                                         Edmund
                                                                            Martin
                                                                            Elizabeth
John Hardwick    =    Elizabeth                                             Margaret
b. 1495/6         dau. of Thomas Leeke                                      Agnes
d. 1528           of Hasland                                                Joan

Elizabeth        Four other daughters    James Hardwick
Countess of Shrewsbury etc               b. 1525; d. 1580/1
b. 1521/2
d. 1608

gentry, and their horizons – social, economic and political – were largely bounded by Scarsdale hundred, the administrative unit that included the whole of north-east Derbyshire, centred on Chesterfield. Not until James Hardwick came of age in 1546 did their position change.

The best picture of James Hardwick's estate, at the end of two decades of purchases, comes from a rental of 1570, which lists lands worth a total of £388 a year. This includes Hardwick Hall and the surrounding park, which was in hand, rather than let to tenants, and so his actual income would have been around £320 a year. This was presumably more than his father had ever enjoyed, but it was small beer compared with the larger gentry estates of the district, much less those of the earls of Shrewsbury. The core of the estate remained Hardwick itself and holdings in the adjoining villages of Hardstoft, Astwith and Heath. James's major purchase in the immediate neighbourhood were the twin manors of Langwith Bassett and Houghton Bassett, bought from a Yorkshire family named Vavasour in 1567; he had also acquired the former Felley priory lands at Houghton Felley (i.e. the southern half of Stony Houghton village), which included premises in Shirebrook and Glapwell. Slightly further afield James

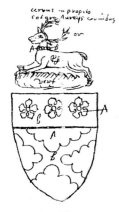

*Figure 14* The arms and crest of the Hardwick family.

*Figure 15*  Extract
from James Hardwick's
rental of 1570, part
of the archive held at
Chatsworth.

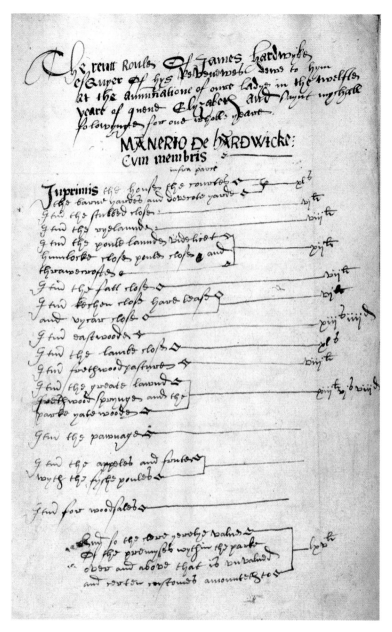

had bought the rectory of Sutton in Ashfield and land in Hucknall
under Huthwaite. There was a handful of estates elsewhere in
Derbyshire (at Winster and Aldwark in the Peak, and Little Hallam
in the south-east of the county) and Nottinghamshire (at Bunny
and Kinoulton, and also Basford rectory), but most of the estate
formed a fairly compact block centred on Hardwick. James also
held some lands in right of his wife (most of which would revert
to her first husband's family at her death) and some leaseholds.

The latter included former chantry land in Chesterfield and the manor of Tibshelf, leased from St Thomas's Hospital in London, which was occupied by his illegitimate son John Hardwick. A couple of small coalpits and some marlpits had been opened at Tibshelf and elsewhere but there is no sign of mining on a large scale. A map of James Hardwick's estate in 1570 shows quite a large number of individual holdings, but most were quite small and not all belonged to him outright.

A rental gives a snapshot picture of the value of an estate and thus some idea of its owner's income before outgoings; it does not provide an overall view of his finances. None of James Hardwick's accounts survive for this period, whereas from the 1590s onwards we have a much better view of both income and expenditure on the Hardwick estate. It is clear from a series of later Chancery actions, however, that James borrowed extensively to fund his purchases. By 1579 his affairs had reached a crisis, and he was obliged to convey his estates to two senior judges, the Lord Chancellor and the Queen's Remembrancer, who were to hold them in trust for his creditors. James is sometimes said to have ended his life 'bankrupt'. Strictly speaking, landowners (as opposed to merchants) could not become bankrupt in the modern sense in this period: more accurately, James's estate was in receivership. This arrangement did not entirely protect him from his creditors and in 1580 James was imprisoned in the London debtors' prison, the Fleet. By this time the position was sufficiently serious for the Lord Chancellor to ask three senior Derbyshire justices of the peace to establish what exactly Hardwick's position was, and whether his estate was, as he claimed, worth £6,000. If the rental of 1570 is any guide, and given that Hardwick made some further purchases after this date, this estimate was probably about right, assuming, as contemporaries generally did, that the estate was worth around fifteen times its annual rental.

The crisis came to a head when James died, apparently still in the Fleet, either in 1580 or early in 1581. He left no legitimate issue, although his son John, who later lived at Williamthorpe, might have had some claim on the estate had it not been so heavily indebted. What were Sir Thomas Bromley, the Lord Chancellor, and Henry Fanshawe, the Queen's Remembrancer, to do as trustees for the creditors?

## BESS OF HARDWICK AND HER FOUR HUSBANDS

A solution was found to the problem created by James Hardwick's death two years later when his estate was purchased by William Cavendish, the second son of Bess and her second husband, also named William Cavendish, the father of all her children. The

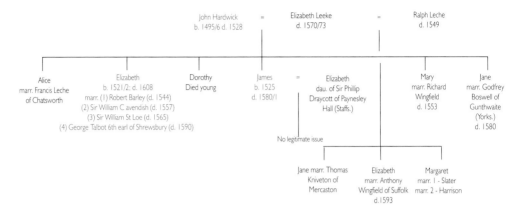

Figure 16  Chart
pedigree of Bess and her
immediate family.

Figure 17  Northaw,
the Hertfordshire
house which Sir William
Cavendish sold in 1552.
He bought estates in
Derbyshire centred on
Chatsworth instead.

younger Cavendish agreed with Bromley and Fanshawe that he
would satisfy Hardwick's remaining creditors and make some
provision for John Hardwick, both of which conditions he fulfilled.
At the same time, he succeeded in keeping intact the block of
land which his uncle had accumulated, and paved the way for his
mother to build two great houses at Hardwick itself. To understand
how, and indeed why, this purchase occurred it is necessary to go
back a generation and look at Bess's career up to the point at which
she was widowed for the last time in 1590.[4]

Bess, born in 1521 or the early months of 1522, was probably her
parents' second or third daughter and was about three years older than
her brother James. In 1543 she married a young man named Robert
Barley, the son of Arthur Barley, whose family had held an estate at

*Figure 18* The remains of Bradgate House near Leicester, seat of the Grey family, where Sir William Cavendish married the widowed Bess in 1547.

Barlow (also known as Barley) on the other side of Chesterfield from Hardwick since the 12th century. The marriage appears to have been arranged for the benefit of the Barley estate. Arthur died before Robert came of age, but Robert also died young, leaving his younger brother as heir, with the prospect of a long wardship and a further claim (from Bess) for a dower income from the family's estate. Bess, left a widow when she was barely 21, sued for dower early in 1545. Rather than the traditional third, she could claim only one ninth (a third of a third), since the estate was already encumbered with payments to Robert's mother and grandmother. Her claim was successful, but she received lands worth only £24 a year, a modest income with which to try to find another husband. The marriage was childless.

Bess remarried in 1547, an event which remains perhaps the greatest unexplained mystery of her life. Her new husband was a senior official of the Royal Household, Sir William Cavendish. The son of an Exchequer official whose ancestors had been London mercers and drapers, William's early career was spent in the Court of Augmentations, dealing with the influx of estates following the dissolution of the monasteries. Acquitting himself well in land management in both England and Ireland, William was rewarded by an appointment, early in 1546, as Treasurer of the Chamber, an office which brought him close to the Crown. He was knighted the same year and also widowed for the second time. As an official at Court, William lived mainly in London but he had some years earlier bought an estate at Northaw, just to the north of the capital, which had previously belonged to St Albans abbey. He had also made other purchases of land elsewhere in Hertfordshire.[5]

In the summer of 1547 Sir William married Bess as his third wife. How did someone in his position come to meet, never mind marry, the daughter of a minor landowner in a county with which he had no personal or professional links? The only clue appears to lie in the place where the marriage took place, Bradgate House in north Leicestershire, then the seat of the branch of the Grey family headed by the marquess of Dorset. Bess may have been in service with Lady Dorset as a gentlewoman attendant, since there was a very distant connection between Bess's mother and the marquess of Dorset's family. Elizabeth Hardwick's father, Thomas Leeke, was related to the head of the Derbyshire branch of the Leeke family, who had acquired their home estate at Sutton by marriage with an heiress of the Sandiacre branch of the Grey family. The common ancestor linking the Sandiacre Greys with the branch to which Dorset belonged lived in the reign of Henry III.

This may have been just enough, given 16th-century ideas of kinship and a pressing need to find a place for a widowed daughter with few other prospects, for Elizabeth to have asked Lady Dorset to take Bess into her household. It has certainly been enough for a succession of Bess's biographers, having placed her in service at Bradgate (for which there is no direct evidence), to have speculated on how she captivated a much older widower anxious to remarry. Bess was in her mid-twenties when she married Cavendish; he was thirty-nine.

## Sir William Cavendish and Derbyshire

The same writers have been quick to credit her feminine charms as the reason why, between 1549 and 1552, Cavendish disposed of his Hertfordshire estate and in its place bought lands in Derbyshire, with which he had no previous connection. Nothing in fact survives to explain the decision. The nucleus of the estate was Chatsworth in the Derwent valley, which had previously belonged to Bess's stepfather's family, the Leches, although it had been acquired by another Derbyshire family, the Agards of Foston, shortly before Cavendish bought the manor in 1549. The following year he purchased the nearby manor of Ashford, in the Wye valley, from Henry Nevile, earl of Westmorland – who was presumably happy to dispose of an isolated estate far from his native county – and the rectory of Edensor, the parish in which Chatsworth lies. Then in 1552 Cavendish sold his remaining Hertfordshire estate, including the house at Northaw, to the Crown in exchange for a large grant of lands, tithes and advowsons (church livings), mostly

owned previously by religious houses, worth a total of £240 a year.
About four fifths of the estate lay in Derbyshire or just over the
Staffordshire border at Tutbury. Some of the purchases were sold on
almost straightaway but what remained, chiefly a group of estates
in the Derwent and Wye valleys around Chatsworth, a second block
of land in mid-Derbyshire around Pentrich that had once belonged
to Darley abbey, and the south-west Derbyshire manors centred on
Tutbury, became the core of the Cavendish family's holdings in the
county for the next 400 years. As well as Chatsworth, some of the
land purchased in 1549-52 still belongs to the estate today.

*Figure 19* Sir William
Cavendish, a portrait
painted *c.*1552, about
the time he moved
from Hertfordshire to
Derbyshire, looking every
inch the successful civil
servant and landowner he
was by this date.

As soon as Sir William acquired Chatsworth, he and Bess began to build a new house there. Most of the work appears to have been supervised by Bess, since her husband continued to live mainly in London. Bess also provided her husband with a large family, three sons and five daughters, of whom all the boys and three of the girls survived to adulthood. Alas, Sir William did not live to see either the new Chatsworth completed or his new family grow up. He died in 1557, possibly a victim of the flu epidemic of that year, leaving Bess with a large number of young children to provide for, and also leaving behind him charges that he owed the Crown more than £5,000 on his accounts as Treasurer of the Chamber.

Cavendish appears not to have made a will, but a few months before his death had settled his estates in conventional fashion for a man with only daughters from his first two marriages and very young sons by his third wife. Chatsworth and most of the rest of his lands were to pass to his eldest son Henry, with the former Darley abbey lands in mid-Derbyshire left to his second son William. It is not clear why no provision was made for his third son, Charles. The settlement on his two sons was subject to a life interest for his widow, whom he may have expected was likely to outlive him. Bess would in any case have had charge of the estate for a lengthy period, since Henry and William, born in 1550 and 1551, were only a few years old at their father's death.

## Bess's Second Widowhood

Like many women in her position, Bess evidently decided that her best course of action when confronted with another early widowhood was to remarry. During her marriage to Sir William Cavendish, when not giving birth or rebuilding Chatsworth, she must have spent some time at Court (although the notion that was she was once a 'lady in waiting' to Queen Elizabeth is mistaken), and her third husband was also from that circle, albeit of a rather different character to Cavendish.

Sir William St Loe, who married Bess as his second wife in 1559, was the head of a long-established Somerset gentry family whose main seat was at Sutton Court, near Bath. In contrast to Cavendish's career as an official, St Loe had been a soldier before he inherited the family's estate. Thereafter he divided his time between county administration in Somerset and service at Court as Captain of the Queen's Guard. He may have been a few years older than Bess, but not half a generation, as Cavendish had been. Like Cavendish (and indeed Bess), St Loe's religious views were strongly Protestant and his family came under something of a cloud during Queen Mary's reign before they re-emerged and enjoyed much better fortune after 1558.[6]

*Figure 20* A characteristically mournful portrait of George Talbot, 6th earl of Shrewsbury, a great magnate who, despite his wealth and power, thought himself the victim of injustice and unfair treatment at the hands of others.

Bess's third marriage gave her the resources to complete the building of the new house at Chatsworth, even though her husband seems to have spent little time in Derbyshire and made few additions to the estate his wife had brought him. The later years of their marriage, which was childless and lasted until St Loe's death in 1565, were dominated by a dispute between Sir William and his younger brother, Edward, who, since St Loe had no children by either of his wives, was his heir. In the early 1560s Edward apparently attempted to poison St Loe and Bess and, as a result, William left Bess his estates, which he was free to dispose of as he wished. Edward challenged this decision in the courts but without success. As a result Bess, unusually for a woman of this period who was not an heiress, secured the outright ownership of the St Loe estates in Somerset and Gloucestershire, estimated in the early 1580s to be worth £700 a year, to add to her dower estate at Barlow and her life interest in her second husband's estate.

For many prospective husbands, an income of perhaps £2,500 a year would have made Bess an attractive prospect on purely mercenary grounds, but this could hardly be said of the man she did marry as her fourth husband. George Talbot, 6th earl of Shrewsbury, was the head of a major peerage family whose members had been Privy Councillors and held other senior offices for generations. More precisely, he was the greatest landowner in the region centred on Sheffield which included north Derbyshire and north Nottinghamshire. Shrewsbury, who succeeded his father in 1560, had been married since 1539 to Gertrude Manners, the eldest daughter of Thomas Manners, 1st earl of Rutland.[7]

## Countess of Shrewsbury

Lady Shrewsbury died in 1566 and, the following year, Bess became the earl's second wife. The two would have known each other, both at Court and in Derbyshire, for many years, although hardly on terms of social or economic equality: Shrewsbury's income in the 1580s was estimated at £10,000 a year. The marriage was not in any a sense a union of dynasties, but the connection between the families was strengthened in 1568 when Bess's eldest son Henry went through a form of marriage with the earl's daughter Grace (then aged about eight), and Shrewsbury's second son Gilbert became espoused to Bess's 12-year-old daughter, Mary. There was, however, no merger of the two estates since Bess was not an heiress; she had a life interest in two pieces of property and outright ownership of a third. No rentals or accounts survive for this land during Bess's fourth marriage. The Talbot estate papers show that Bess's lands were at no stage incorporated into the administrative

*Figure 21*  A re-construction drawing of Sheffield Manor, the house on the outskirts of the town which was the administrative centre of the earls of Shrewsbury's great estates in south Yorkshire, Derbyshire and Nottinghamshire.

system centred on Sheffield Manor, although the earl became entitled to the income from Bess's estates once they were married.[8]

The three best known aspects of Bess's fourth marriage are her husband's long and unwelcome custodianship of the imprisoned Mary Queen of Scots, the estrangement between Bess and her husband which became an open rift in 1584, and her rebuilding of her family seat at Hardwick in the later 1580s. The second, rather than the third, of these has most bearing on the history of the Hardwick estate; Mary, it might be added, never visited Hardwick, except in the minds of 19th-century romantic writers.

Despite the well-documented later problems, the marriage appears to have got off to a good start. Although their own marriage was childless, both Bess and George had children from previous marriages. Of Bess's children (all from her second marriage), Henry's position was helped by his marriage to Shrewsbury's daughter Grace, and Mary married Grace's brother Gilbert. There remained, however, Bess's two younger sons to be provided for. Born the sons of a gentleman, they were now the stepsons of an earl. In 1572, apparently out of a genuine wish to give the two boys the status they deserved (although he later bitterly regretted the decision), Shrewsbury conveyed the lands he held in right of his wife to the use of William and Charles Cavendish, who came of age in 1571 and 1572 respectively. This settlement was to have consequences which Shrewsbury can hardly have foreseen but were to be crucial for the history of the Hardwick estate from 1572 until the death of Bess in 1608 and her son William in 1626.

As soon as he turned 21 and acquired this source of income, William in particular appears to have exploited his position to the full. According to lists prepared by the earl's officials in 1584, which were not seriously challenged by Bess and her sons, William spent over £25,000 in 12 years buying estates in Derbyshire, Nottinghamshire and Staffordshire. By far the largest single purchase was the £9,500 he laid out in 1583 to buy James Hardwick's lands; indeed it may have been this event which finally provoked Shrewsbury to make his estrangement from Bess public. William further increased his income by his marriage to Anne Keighley, who was coheiress with her younger sister not only to the manor of Keighley, where the family had originated, but also estates in Lancashire, where they had lived for some generations. Apart from this lucrative marriage, where the money to buy land on this scale had come from was unclear at the time and remains uncertain today: Shrewsbury claimed Bess had been taking money from his estates and giving it to her sons to buy land in their names, since as a married woman she could not own property herself. In 1584 the earl alleged that his wife had an income of over £5,000 a year, some of which came from a Crown lease of Peak Forest, Shottle and Postern and some from James Hardwick's estate, both of which formally belonged to her son William. Shrewsbury claimed that William had an income of about £700 a year from the estates he had bought since 1572, besides that which he had from his wife's lands, his involvement in lead smelting, and his money lending.

The problem, as the earl realised, was that Bess and William, assisted to some extent by William's younger brother Charles, had been working together to build up an estate and it was difficult to decide, then as now, how the income from this land was divided between the three of them. What is clear is that by 1584 the lands built up by James Hardwick around the nucleus inherited from his father had passed into Bess's control and had been augmented by purchases by William Cavendish. At the same time, thanks to the settlement of 1572, Bess had a considerable income from lands she held as the result of her three earlier marriages.

It was this independent income that enabled Bess to go ahead with the reconstruction of her family's house at Hardwick, several years before Shrewsbury's death. Nothing is known for certain of earlier houses at Hardwick, or whether James Hardwick began to build a new house there in keeping with his increased wealth. On the other hand, the recent conservation of the ruins of the Old Hall has provided an opportunity to re-examine the surviving fabric in detail, which has led to the conclusion that in their alignment the south and west walls of the hall predate Bess's campaign of building in the 1580s and could belong to James's time. The fact that the various sections of the Old Hall are not aligned symmetrically one with another may also be evidence that some of them stand on the foundations of older buildings. Essentially Bess's rebuilding involved adding two substantial and roughly balancing wings at either end of the hall. At the top of each of them, above three storeys of comparatively low rooms, were a series of immense, lofty state

# Symbols of Regional Power

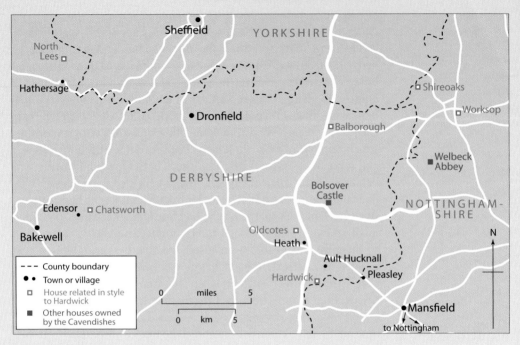

Figure A  *Midlands houses (shown in orange) of the 16th and early 17th centuries which share with Hardwick a tall silhouette and compact plan. This distinctive regional style, perhaps partly inspired by Tudor royal palaces, was developed by the architect-mason Robert Smythson.*

As soon as Bess separated from her husband, the earl of Shrewsbury, she began to build for herself at Hardwick. Her two houses there conform in size and sophistication to the kind of prodigiously magnificent houses built by Elizabethan courtiers such as Lord Burghley, but they also belong to a distinctive local type which proclaimed Bess's Shrewsbury associations – associations loudly broadcast by the huge 'ES' monograms ornamenting the parapet. Bess had had recent experience of building on a grand scale at Chatsworth, and perhaps also with her husband's Worksop Manor in Nottinghamshire, begun in the early 1580s. Both Chatsworth and Worksop were exceptionally tall, perhaps in emulation of Henry VIII's palaces such as Nonsuch and Richmond in Surrey. At Hardwick, Bess continued to experiment with stacking rooms high. In both houses the state rooms were placed on the topmost floors, as they were at Worksop, and reached by dramatic ceremonial staircases. Worksop Manor was a hunting lodge and neither it nor Hardwick overlooked extensive formal gardens; instead they captured views of a hunting park, which is still the setting at Hardwick.

The regional style followed at both halls seems to have been inspired by the work of Robert Smythson, the most famous of the few Elizabethan architectural designers we know by name and from whose hand we have design drawings. The Hardwick accounts give circumstantial evidence that Smythson was involved with the design of the second hall. By comparing it with other houses with which he was involved, such as Longleat in Wiltshire, Wollaton Hall in Nottinghamshire and Worksop Manor, we can recognise a consistent approach to planning, structure and style. The same traits are shared by nearby Barlborough Hall, North Lees Hall, also in Derbyshire, and by Shireoaks Hall and the so-called Worksop Manor Lodge in Nottinghamshire. All were built in the 1580s and 1590s. Whether courtiers like the Talbots or gentry like the Rodeses of Barlborough, these families advertised their status and social connections, as well as their wealth, by means of novel and very distinctive architecture. Their houses are very different from the spreading courtyard mansions built closer to London by other Elizabethan courtiers.

Figure B *Barlborough Hall was built in the 1580s by Francis Rodes who, like Bess's father, was a member of the gentry rather than the aristocracy. When building his 'high house' with a compact plan, he surely must have looked to the work of the earl of Shrewsbury at Worksop Manor (below). There the clustered top-floor state rooms were clearly expressed on the outside.*

Figure C *Worksop Manor, Nottinghamshire, built for the earl of Shrewsbury, c.1580 and probably with the close involvement of his wife, Bess.*

Figure D *West front of Hardwick Hall.*

Elizabeth Williamson

*Figure 22*  The ruins of the Old Hall at Hardwick, which probably incorporate a house begun by James Hardwick, to which Bess made radical alterations in the 1580s but then abandoned in favour of building the New Hall just north of it.

rooms, lit by towering windows. One wing has a tower six storeys high, the other had shallow projecting bays running all the way up, with the unique feature of two full-scale great chambers (the Hill Great Chamber and the Forest Great Chamber) at the west and east ends of the house. The other feature of the Old Hall, which is uncommon in houses of this period, was the way in which the hall ran from front to back across the short axis of the house, instead of being arranged longitudinally. Bess was to carry this arrangement over into the New Hall at Hardwick, built in the 1590s.[9]

## Bess: The Final Widowhood

Although the dispute of 1584 was patched up through the good offices of Queen Elizabeth's minister Lord Burghley, there was no real reconciliation between Shrewsbury and Bess before his death in 1590. Bess was now an enormously wealthy widow, entitled to a dower income amounting to a third of her late husband's estate, or about £3,000 a year. She received up to twice that figure from her other estates (the Barley dower lands, the Cavendish lands, the 'Western' (i.e. St Loe) lands, and the lands purchased on her behalf by her sons in the 1570s and early 1580s), giving her a total income

*Figure 23*  Plaster overmantel of the Forest Great Chamber in the ruins of the Old Hall. A stag was used in the Hardwick crest and was much used by Bess in the decoration of her houses.

of at least £7,000 a year and in some years almost £10,000. Ironically, she now had nearly the same income as her last husband had enjoyed in the 1580s, whereas his son and eventual heir, Gilbert Talbot, the 7th earl of Shrewsbury, who was both Bess's stepson and son-in-law, saw his own resources reduced by the obligation to pay Bess's dower income. Although the Shrewsbury estates centred on Sheffield Manor remained largely intact until after Earl Gilbert's death in 1616, he was not the power in the land his father had been. On two occasions he sold outlying estates, those at Welbeck Abbey and Bolsover, to his brother-in-law Charles Cavendish, possibly because he wished to increase his income. These in turn became the nucleus of the holdings, mainly in Nottinghamshire and Derbyshire, of the Welbeck branch of the Cavendish family, which by the mid-17th century rivalled those of the Hardwick and Chatsworth branch.[10]

Although Bess was nearly 70 when she was widowed for the last time, she clearly remained active for some years after 1590. She played no part in public life and visited London only once, in 1591-2, staying at Shrewsbury House in Chelsea. Otherwise she lived at Hardwick, where, as soon as she had completed the rebuilding of the Old Hall, she appears to have commissioned (or at least consulted) Robert Smythson, then at the height of his fame as an architect of great country houses, especially in the region to which Hardwick belonged, concerning the design of a completely new mansion. This she set about erecting a short distance from the Old Hall, still on the edge of the escarpment overlooking the Doe Lea valley, so that it could be seen from miles around, and from which she could look out over her estates.[11]

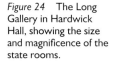

*Figure 24*  The Long Gallery in Hardwick Hall, showing the size and magnificence of the state rooms.

Unlike the Old Hall, which seems to have grown piecemeal, probably around an existing building, the New Hall was built from scratch to a single design. Apart from sympathetic modernisation in the mid-19th century by the 6th duke of Devonshire, which affected the service rooms and farm buildings more than the principal reception rooms and chambers, the building has not been greatly altered since it was completed. The New Hall, like the Old Hall, was laid out around a two-storey hall arranged transversely across the centre of the house. On either side of the hall were symmetrical ranges of service rooms on the ground floor, the main living rooms on the first floor, and a long gallery and state rooms on the second floor. At either end of the building, towers rose by a further storey, giving access to roof-top walkways. The main range had a balustraded pediment; the roofs of the towers were decorated with Bess's initials 'ES', surmounted by a countess's coronet. Outside, the house was flanked by enclosed courtyards.

Bess began building the New Hall at the end of 1590, within months of her husband's death, and the shell was complete by 1593. She moved into her new house in 1597, although finishing work on the interior continued for at some time afterwards. Bess did not abandon the Old Hall once its successor was ready for occupation; indeed some rooms in the Old Hall remained habitable until the end of the 18th century. At first sight this may seem odd: the Old Hall hardly improves the setting of the New Hall and one might have expected Bess to have dismantled the building

*Figure 25* Ground-floor plan of the Old Hall, showing the asymmetrical layout which probably resulted from incorporating an earlier house, and the great hall entered at one end rather than on one of the long sides.

**Ground-floor plan**

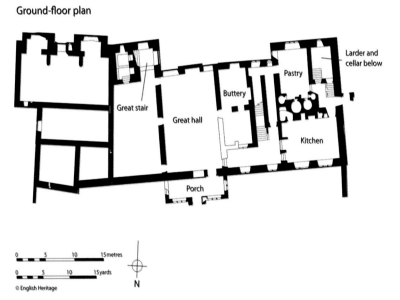

*Figure 26* Plans of the
New Hall, a development
within a more regular
outline of some of the
ideas tried out at the
Old Hall. Bess's private
apartments were on
the first floor, with state
rooms for entertaining
right at the top
of the house.

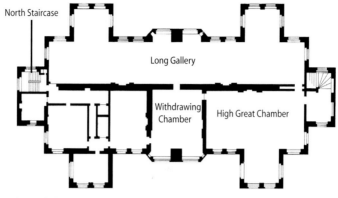

North Staircase

Long Gallery

Withdrawing Chamber

High Great Chamber

Second Floor

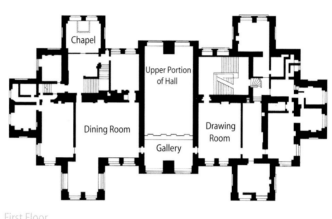

Chapel

Upper Portion of Hall

Dining Room

Drawing Room

Gallery

First Floor

N

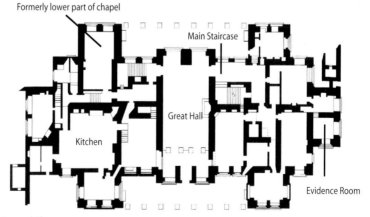

Formerly lower part of chapel

Main Staircase

Great Hall

Kitchen

Evidence Room

Ground Floor

*Figure 27* Monument in Ault Hucknall church to Anne Keighley, first wife of Bess's son, William Cavendish, and their four children.

and used the materials for the New Hall. The main reason why the older house was retained, leaving aside the fact that most of the structure was barely 10 years old, seems to be that the New Hall was not especially large for the size of household Bess maintained, even as an elderly widow. The extra space which the Old Hall provided was needed, even after the New Hall was complete, probably mainly as accommodation for retainers and guests.

## The New Hall and Oldcotes

Bess shared both the old and new Hardwick Halls with her second son William, who never really left home; they did not, it should be added, divide the two mansions between them, with Bess in the New Hall and William in the Old Hall. Whereas Henry had settled at Tutbury soon after he married in 1568 and Charles, after his second marriage in 1592 to a daughter of Lord Ogle, made his home at Welbeck, William and his first wife, Anne Keighley, lived with his mother throughout their married life. During the 1590s, while she was still busy with the New Hall at Hardwick, Bess commissioned Smythson to design a second, smaller house to be erected alongside the existing farmhouse at Oldcotes, in the north of Heath parish, on land acquired as part of her purchase of the manor of Stainsby in 1593. This was intended to be a home for William and Anne. In the event Anne died in 1598, at about the time Oldcotes was ready for occupation, and William never moved in, either as a widower or with his second wife, Elizabeth Wortley, whom he married in 1604. William and Elizabeth continued to share Hardwick until Bess died four years later, when it came to them outright. By this time William had a house (rather than lodgings) in London, where he and his wife spent much of their time between late autumn and late spring each year. William completed Oldcotes but never lived there and the house was left in charge of a bailiff, who ran the place as a demesne farm. It remained something of a white elephant for the estate until William's grandson, the 3rd earl of Devonshire, sold the house and some adjoining land in 1641. Bess's mansion at Oldcotes was demolished *c.*1710 and some of the masonry was used to build High House, elsewhere on the estate; the earlier building at Oldcotes survives as a farmhouse.[12]

Apart from building the New Hall, Bess's other main activity in the 1590s and 1600s was the purchase of further lands, all of which were settled on her second son William. By this date she appears to have given up any hope that Henry, her eldest son, would be a worthy heir to his father. This was partly because he had no legitimate offspring by his wife Grace, but a large brood of illegitimate children, and partly because he was what Bess described as an 'ill-manager' of his estates and always short of money.

*Figure 28* A drawing in the Smythson Collection which may (by comparison with a 17th-century sketch of the house as built) be a design for Oldcotes. This was the mansion near Heath built by Bess for her son William and his first wife, who never really used the house.

William, on the other hand, had worked closely with his mother since the 1570s in acquiring land and exploiting its resources to the full. He in turn was presumably anxious not to fall foul of Bess and for this reason, if no other, was prepared to share her house, even as a married man in his fifties. Bess's local purchases in this period included the manor of Stainsby and three smaller estates a few miles to the north, at Woodthorpe (in Staveley), Romeley (in Clowne) and Oxcroft (in Bolsover). Further afield she bought Wetherby and three nearby manors in the West Riding, and three other manors (Lartington, Cotherstone and Cleasby) in the North Riding, close to the County Durham border. She also acquired the manor of Claxby (near Alford) in Lincolnshire. Her other purchases were of rectories, rather than manors, which brought a useful tithe income as well as the right to appoint the incumbent (the advowson), which was itself a saleable asset. The list included Hathersage in the Peak and Chaddesden near Derby; two groups of advowsons in Nottinghamshire, one near Retford and the other near Nottingham; Thornton in Lincolnshire; Hatfield in the Don valley in south Yorkshire; and Prestwold, Buckminster and Sewstern in Leicestershire. All these new acquisitions, like those she had held for some time, were administered by bailiffs who accounted to Bess's receiver at Hardwick. As a result, by 1608 the New Hall at Hardwick had become the administrative hub of an estate which stretched from the Tees Valley to the Vale of Belvoir, although most of the holdings were less than 20 miles from the mansion.[13]

# Two Elizabethan Interiors: Inventories and Accounts

Although the structure and plan of Hardwick Hall remain largely unchanged, the apparently authentic Elizabethan interior decoration is largely a romantic re-creation by the 6th duke of Devonshire in the mid-19th century. After 1700, when Chatsworth became the focus of Cavendish life, how the house was used and furnished changed. The duke created his artistic effects by bringing many 16th- and 17th-century pieces from Chatsworth, including those moved there from Hardwick after Bess's death and also Chatsworth furnishings she had inherited from her Cavendish husband. The National Trust has refined the presentation but has maintained the collection as an example of the duke's taste, which belonged to the revival of interest amongst country house owners in the venerable mansions they had inherited.

Evidence of how rooms were furnished in Bess's time has come from the inventories of Hardwick and Chatsworth compiled to accompany her will, drawn up in 1601. Many such inventories exist but few can be linked with so many surviving items. As with all inventories of this period, rooms are given their contemporary names (often after occupants, function or predominant furnishing) and so not all can be identified. They were also recorded in an unknown and not necessarily logical order. In order to interpret the use and meaning of rooms and furnishings, we need to understand how households were run and hospitality conducted. This type of research has been carried out at Hardwick since the 1970s. It contributed significantly to a revolution in country-house studies, encapsulated by Mark Girouard's influential book, *Life in the English Country House*, first published in 1978.

The Hardwick inventories give a vivid picture of how richly Bess's houses were furnished with tapestries and embroidered textiles as well as wooden furniture, how life was conducted (with warm hangings against the cold, for example), and about personal taste. For example, both old and new halls had great chambers, large and elaborately decorated rooms for formal entertaining of favoured guests. The Old Hall (below) had two, one at each end of the house. The plasterwork

Figure A    *View over the estate and beyond from the windows of the Hill Great Chamber in Hardwick Old Hall.*

Figure B  *Hardwick Hall, the High Great Chamber. Guests would have enjoyed the contrast between the artificial, classical hunting scene round the room and the view of the hunting park seen from the vast windows.*

in the Hill Great Chamber was made according to the building accounts by Abraham Smith, has classical motifs probably selected by Bess or one of her circle; patrons, better educated and more conversant with fashionable buildings and learning than even the most skilled workmen, were closely involved with the design of their houses. The theme of the Old Hall's Forest Great Chamber was repeated by Smith in the Old Hall's High Great Chamber of the New Hall, where the brightly coloured scenes of the hunting goddess Diana and her court were chosen perhaps as a compliment to Elizabeth I. The Brussels tapestries, also with classical scenes, have hung below them since at least 1601. Bess certainly sat in state under a canopy, although that in the new Hall's great chamber was made for Countess Christian and placed there by the 6th duke. By entertaining visitors in such a setting, Bess made plain her importance as countess of Shrewsbury, founder of her own, Cavendish dynasty, and grandmother of a possible future queen, Arbella Stuart.

Sources: D.N. Durant and P. Riden (eds), *The Building Accounts of Hardwick Hall, Part 1: the Old Hall, 1587-91*, Derbyshire Record Society, 4 (1980); *The Building Accounts of Hardwick Hall, Part 2: the New Hall, 1591-8*, Derbyshire Record Society, 9 (1984); *Of Household Stuff: the 1601 inventories of Bess of Hardwick* (National Trust, 2001).

Elizabeth Williamson

## The Final Triumph

Bess died in February 1608, at Hardwick. She was buried three
months later in great state, beneath a monument designed by
Smythson, at All Saints', the largest of the five parish churches of
Derby. She had, a few years earlier, endowed a hospital at Derby,
but otherwise had no close links with the county town. As an
elderly widow, she did not go to Derby for quarter sessions, the
assizes or Parliamentary elections, as William did, and no member
of the family owned any land in the borough.

Bess left a long and much amended will, supported by a detailed
inventory of the contents of both houses at Hardwick, but its
provisions concerning the lands which were hers to dispose of were
straightforward: all her purchased lands went to William, apart
from the Western Lands, which passed to her youngest son Charles.
Her two dower estates, the legacy of her first and last marriages,
reverted in both cases to the 7th earl of Shrewsbury, whose
father had, just before his death, bought what remained of the
impoverished Barley family's lands. Finally, the lands accumulated
by her second husband, Sir William Cavendish, passed in
accordance with his settlement of 1557 mainly to their eldest son
Henry (including the mansion and demesnes at Chatsworth), apart
from the mid-Derbyshire estate around Pentrich.[14]

This was not quite the end of the story. Almost as soon as their
mother was buried William wrote to his elder brother, Henry, offering
to purchase from him those of their father's estates which had just
passed to him. In return for a cash sum immediately, an annual
income for the remaining years of his life, and an annuity thereafter
for his widow, Grace (who in the event survived until 1640), William

*Figure 29*   The effigy
of Elizabeth, countess
of Shrewsbury,
incorporated in her
elaborate monument in
All Saints', Derby (now
the cathedral).

would have all Henry's lands after his death, apart from a small estate at Tutbury itself. It was, as both men probably realised, an offer Henry could not afford to reject. He was, as always, short of money; and although he now had the mansion at Chatsworth, its contents had been left to William, and so the house would have passed to him unfurnished. Although suspicious (with good reason) that his brother was making a hard bargain from which William, rather than Henry or his wife, would be the main beneficiary, he agreed to convey most of the estates that came to him under the settlement of 1557 to William, the conveyance to take effect at his death.

As a result of this manoeuvre, when Henry Cavendish died in 1616 William acquired almost all their father's estates in Derbyshire and elsewhere, including most crucially the mansion at Chatsworth. By this device, not only was his income greatly increased but he had secured all three great houses in Derbyshire built by his mother over a 40-year period. It was by any standards a considerable achievement for a second son whose father had died when he was six, leaving debts of over £5,000.

Nor was this William's only purchase in this period. Even before his mother died, he had begun to add to his own estate. In 1599 he bought the site and demesnes of Glastonbury Abbey in Somerset and in about 1604 the manor of Haddlesey, near Selby in the West Riding. Further acquisitions followed as his income rose after his mother's death, mainly of estates south of the Trent, where the family became major landowners for the first time. These included manors at Sawtry (in Huntingdonshire), Hundon (in Suffolk) and Evington (in Leicestershire), as well as the site and demesnes of Leicester Abbey. After briefly renting one house in Hertfordshire and owning another for a short time, William purchased the Buckinghamshire manors of Latimer and Chesham, which included a house (at Latimer) that was a convenient base for short visits to London, much as Northaw had been for his father. He also bought a much larger house in London, on Aldersgate, to the north of the City, in place of the house in Holborn he had owned since shortly before his second marriage.[15]

Almost all William's growing wealth (over 90 per cent) came from land, although he was also involved in several overseas trading companies, especially the East India Company and the Somer Islands Company, established to develop Bermuda, and for a few years in the 1600s had a lead smelter at Barlow. His increased income was reflected in his his rising status in society. In 1605, a year after he married the widow of Richard Wortley of Wortley in south Yorkshire (who brought him a significant additional income from her dower lands), William was created Baron Cavendish of Hardwick. This apparently came about through the intercession with the king of William's niece, Arbella, the daughter of his sister

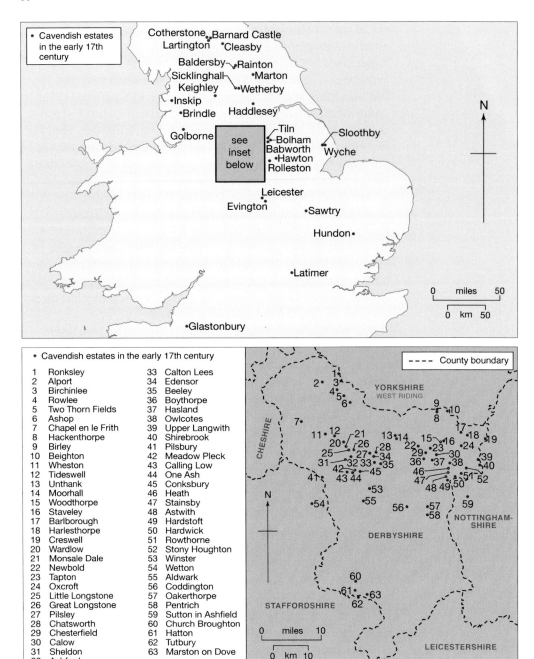

*Figure 30* Map showing the estates of the 1st earl of Devonshire.

Elizabeth and her husband Charles Stuart, earl of Lennox. Through her father's family, Arbella was a close relation of James I. Although this proximity to the Crown may have helped William, it conferred no benefit on Arbella, whose life was a genuine tragedy which has attracted even more attention from romantic biographers than that of her grandmother Bess. More mundanely, William paid £2,000 for his peerage. This represented a substantial step up for a man who had never (unlike his brother Charles) been knighted. Further reward was to come in 1618, when Cavendish paid £10,000 for an earldom, one of four sold by the Crown that year. The title he chose was Devon or Devonshire, apparently simply because it was vacant, whereas the Stanley family had long been earls of Derby.

Even after his promotion, William played little part in public life. Like any great magnate, even one whose family had risen to that position within a single generation, he attended the House of Lords, was at Court from time to time, and exchanged New Year gifts with the king. But he held no office, other than the Derbyshire lord lieutenancy, and left politics to his son and heir William, who was an active member of the Commons, especially in connection with colonial affairs, and lived in London rather than the country.[16]

William Cavendish, 1st earl of Devonshire, died in March 1626 and was buried at Edensor beneath a monument that also commemorates his brother Henry. At the time of his death William possessed lands worth over £16,000 a year, although some of the estate was in hand and his rental income was about £12,000. He owned three great houses in Derbyshire, a town house in London and another in Buckinghamshire. Just over half the estate lay in Derbyshire and the adjoining counties of Staffordshire and Nottinghamshire; the rest was divided between about a dozen other counties.

Perhaps more important than its geographical distribution, given the traditional view that the architect of the Cavendish family's fortune was Bess of Hardwick, are the origins of the estate. At the time of his death about twenty per cent of the earl's total rental (excluding lands held on lease or in right of his wife, and a few for which the origin cannot be traced) was represented by lands bought by Sir William Cavendish between 1549 and 1557, and about ten per cent by the purchases he had made on behalf of his mother between 1572 and 1584. The most important of these was the estate built up by James Hardwick. A quarter came from lands bought by Bess in her last widowhood, but the lion's share, some 47 per cent, was from lands he had bought himself or acquired with his first wife. Clearly Bess is an important figure in the history of the Hardwick estate in the 16th century, at least between the early 1580s and her death, but proper credit should also be given to her second husband, her brother and her second son. All three played some part in the transformation of Hardwick, within barely two generations, from the seat of a minor gentry family into the centre of one of the greatest peerage estates in England. Once it had acquired this standing, Hardwick was to retain it for another two generations, until the end of the 17th century, when the changing circumstances (and tastes) of the Cavendish family meant that Hardwick's status would decline.[17]

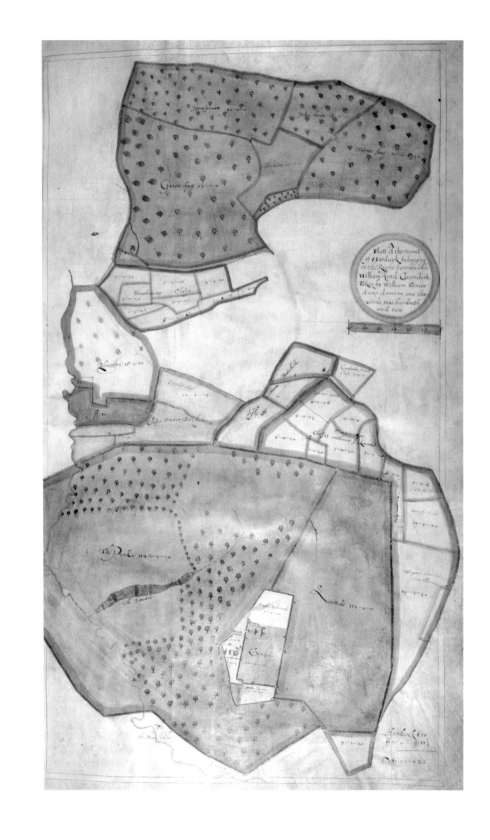

A
Platt of the mannor
of Hardwick belonging
to the Right honorable
William Lord Cavendish.
Taken by William Senior
Anno domini one thou-
sande sixe hundreth
and ten

# Chapter 3

# Hardwick in the Seventeenth Century

Between the completion of the New Hall in the late 1590s and the end of the 17th century Hardwick was both the main administrative centre of the Cavendish estate and the family's principal country residence. Once the rebuilding of Chatsworth was completed in about 1694, however, Hardwick was occupied only occasionally by a family who spent most of the year in London. In 1700 the post of Derbyshire receiver, the chief administrative officer for the estate in the north of England, who had generally been based at Hardwick, was abolished. Thereafter the estate as a whole was run mainly from London and the Derbyshire portion administered from Chatsworth, not Hardwick. These changes give the 17th century both a special importance in the history of Hardwick and a certain unity.

## FAMILY FORTUNES

Hardwick's position as an administrative centre did not change a great deal between Bess's death in 1608 and 1700, but its role as a family home varied according to the family's circumstances. After his mother died, Lord Cavendish (as her son William was known between 1605 and 1618) and his second wife continued to make Hardwick their main Derbyshire residence. They never used Oldcotes, which was presumably regarded as too small, and spent only a few summers at Chatsworth after it came into William's possession following the death of his elder brother Henry in 1616. They did, on the other hand, spend about two thirds of each year in London, generally from the late autumn until the late spring, with their visits sometimes flanked, or interrupted, by short stays at Latimer House (or 'Latimers', as it was called in this period), near Chesham in south Buckinghamshire. Cavendish's eldest son, also named William, who turned 18 the year Bess died, seems to have lived entirely in London after returning from a European tour, but not at his father's house in Aldersgate Street. His sister Frances lived at home until her marriage in 1608, as did their half-brother John, the only child of William's second marriage, who died aged about ten and was buried at Chesham.[18]

After the 1st earl of Devonshire (as William Cavendish became in 1618) died in 1626 his widow, Countess Elizabeth, seems to

*Figure 32* Shrewsbury
House on Cheyne Walk
in Chelsea, which the
earls of Shrewsbury used
as a convenient retreat
from London. After Bess's
husband, the 6th earl,
died in 1590 she used
Shrewsbury House on
her last visit to the capital
in 1591-2. Some years
later her son William
bought the house from
his brother-in-law, the
7th earl of Shrewsbury,
and after William died in
1626 his widow, Elizabeth,
lived there.

have spent most of her time at Shrewsbury House in Chelsea,
which her husband had bought from the 7th earl of Shrewsbury,
although she also had the use of Latimers. Shrewsbury House
was sold after Elizabeth died in 1642, when Latimers reverted
to the 3rd earl. The 2nd earl outlived his father by barely two
years, dying heavily in debt in the summer of 1628. Although he
is usually dismissed in accounts of the family as an extravagant
wastrel, compared with his father and his own son and successor,

*Figure 33* Chart
pedigree: the descendants
of Sir William and Lady
Cavendish. The heirs to
the estates are shown
in red.

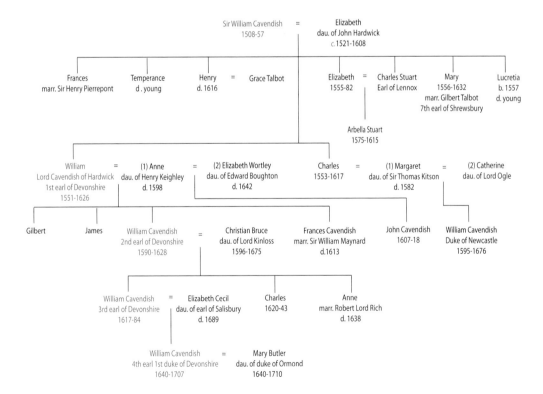

both of whom are seen as prudent managers of their estates, the 2nd earl clearly grasped that he had to act to stabilise the family's finances, not least because of the need to make substantial dower payments to his stepmother, Countess Elizabeth. He immediately sold his father's stock in the East India Company, presumably to raise some cash, and then, in the final months of his life, steered through Parliament in the face of significant opposition a bill enabling him to sell some of the settled estate to clear his debts. His father, although he had been taking out short-term, unsecured loans towards the end of his life, probably to fund purchases of land, had died free of debt.[19]

The 2nd earl's death complicated the financial position. Apart from leaving large personal debts, Earl William had bought a new London house, Fisher's Folly on Bishopsgate, later known as Devonshire House, since his father's London house on Aldersgate Street was part of Countess Elizabeth's jointure estate. Worse still, the head of the family was now an 11-year-old boy, whose mother, the 2nd earl's widow, Countess Christian, was entitled to a dower income from her late husband's estate. The family were thus facing something of a crisis, but Countess Christian devoted the following ten years to solving the problems she inherited. Christian divided her time between Devonshire House in London and the country, although at which house in Derbyshire she spent most time is unclear. Some, but not all, of the lands scheduled in the 2nd earl's Act of 1628 were sold, including the trio of small manors to the north of Hardwick at Woodthorpe, Romeley and Oxcroft, but the core estate in Derbyshire, including all three mansions, remained intact. Nor did the family have to sell their house at Leicester, which Countess Christian used for a time as a dower house after her son, the 3rd earl, came of age in 1638.[20]

Soon after his coming of age the 3rd earl replaced his cousin, William Cavendish of Welbeck, by then earl of Newcastle, as lord lieutenant of Derbyshire, an office his father and grandfather had held jointly between 1619 and 1628. He also played an active part in the House of Lords. At the outbreak of the Civil War in 1642 he joined the king at York and was one of a number of earls ordered by Parliament to be impeached. Faced with this threat, Devonshire left the country with his wife Elizabeth Cecil, a daughter of the 2nd earl of Salisbury, and infant son (the future 1st duke), and spent the next three years on the Continent. In 1644, and possibly at other times during this period, he was at Rouen. He left behind his mother, Countess Christian, and younger brother Charles, who died fighting for the Royalists at Gainsborough in 1643. No contemporary explanation for the earl's action, which on the face of it might seem defeatist or cowardly, appears to survive, although it was presumably taken in the hope of avoiding damage to his estates. Chatsworth passed into Parliamentary hands early in the Civil War, and was not recovered for several years; Hardwick, where the servants were specifically ordered by Charles Cavendish to stop preparing earthworks from which to defend the house, was also garrisoned by Parliament for a time. Neither appears to have seen any actual fighting or to have been damaged during the war.[21]

After he returned to England the 3rd earl seems to have devoted himself single-mindedly to the restoration of his fortunes. Unlike his mother, who was a minor Royalist plotter in the 1650s, he took no part in politics. Instead, he concentrated on paying off debt and setting the estate administration to rights after three years in which it had lacked his leadership. Almost all the tenants seem to have been given new leases, replacing those issued by the 2nd earl in 1627, most of which would have expired in 1648.

When the king returned in 1660, Devonshire and his wife travelled to London to welcome him; they were also in London for the coronation the following year. But the 3rd earl was not among then former Royalists who sought office or reward from Charles II: he served briefly as a commissioner for trade in 1667-8 but was not active in the Lords. He divided his time between London and the country, but he and his family did not invariably go up to London in the late autumn for the winter season and stay in town until the spring or early summer. Some years he spent entirely in the country, partly at Hardwick and partly at Chatsworth.

Throughout the later years of his life the 3rd earl's main interest appears to have been the efficient and economical working of his estate: his signature appears on literally hundreds of pages of surviving accounts, showing that he meticulously checked his officials' work, often down to quite a junior level, and did not merely accept summaries placed before him by his auditor. He frequently queried errors in arithmetic or what he saw as excessive expenditure on a particular item.

The 3rd earl did not add greatly to the estate in the way in which his grandfather did. In 1662 he was able to buy the manor of Hartington in the Peak from the Crown (which the family had leased for some years) and also purchased the manor of Staveley, to the north of Hardwick, from after the death of Lord Frescheville, which occurred in 1681. He did not carry out any major building works at either Derbyshire house, although in the 1670s a number of statues were bought for the gardens at Chatsworth. In London the family lived in a succession of rented houses: Devonshire House in the City was still occupied by Countess Christian, who also had a country seat at Roehampton, and the house on Aldersgate Street had long been sold off.[22]

The 3rd earl died at Roehampton in 1684. His son, with whom he had been on very bad terms, appears to have been quite different in character from his father. Active in the Commons from his twenties, the 4th earl became a prominent figure in the Country party opposed to James II and took a leading part in the Glorious Revolution of 1688. His reward was high office under William III, including periods as a lord commissioner authorised to act in the king's name during his absence in the Netherlands, and, in 1694, promotion to a dukedom. He appears not to have had his father's close interest in the day-to-day running of the estate and, both before and after he succeeded to the earldom, lived mainly in London. The family sold Devonshire House on Bishopsgate following the death of Countess Christian in 1675 and, after occupying several West End houses for short periods in the

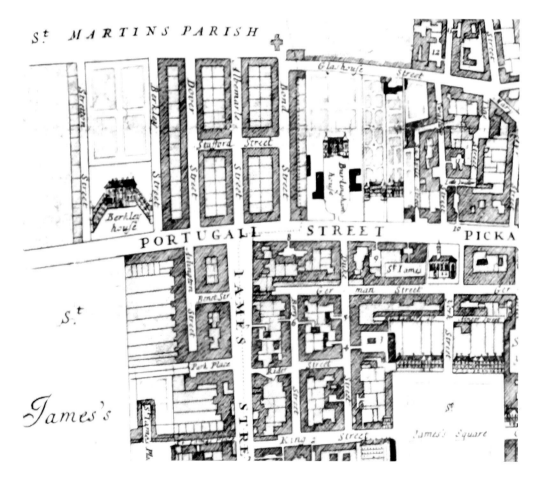

*Figure 34* A section of Blome's *Map of the parish of St James* (1689) showing the mansions along Portugal Street (later Piccadilly). They include Berkeley House, which was bought by the Cavendishes and became Devonshire House.

# Managing a Great Estate

One of the reasons why the Cavendish estate proved so durable was that, during the period in which it was built up by Bess of Hardwick and her son William, an efficient administrative system was developed. It proved sufficiently flexible to survive, modernised but essentially unchanged, until after the First World War, and for most of this long period is well documented by surviving records.

Bess ran her growing estate on the same lines as other great landowners, with a senior official, the receiver, based at Hardwick, to whom the bailiffs in charge of individual manors accounted. The receiver reported to Bess, who audited her accounts herself every week. Her son William, the 1st earl of Devonshire, adopted a more complex system. He had two receivers, one at Hardwick and the other in London, who were co-equal and worked separately, whereas most families had a single receiver-general controlling all receipts and disbursements. Both sets of accounts were audited by the earl. Both receivers had a number of sub-accountants who reported to them, in addition to

Figure A  *One of two overmantels on the second floor of the Old Hall. Research by David Durant and Mark Girouard concluded that these rooms belonged to upper servants in Bess of Hardwick's household. The grandness of their decoration shows the status that employees such as William Reason, Bess's receiver, enjoyed.*

Figure B  *The 17th-century stables and coachhouse (altered in the 19th century) in the service court at Hardwick. The master of the horse, based in London, was in charge of the stables, including coaches as well as horses, in both London and Derbyshire.*

Figure C   *The* Hardwick Inn, *which lies at the gates of Hardwick Park, was used as the estate office in the 17th century.*

the bailiffs of the various 'collections', as the individual accounting units were known. In Derbyshire these included the housekeepers in charge of Hardwick and Chatsworth, and the husbandmen who looked after the home farms at both houses.

The main change during the 17th century, as on other estates of similar size, was the rise in importance of the steward, who travelled with the family as they moved between London and the country. By the 3rd earl's time the steward was the head of a large spending department, funded mainly by the London receiver. Towards the end of the 17th century, when the family lived mostly in London, the work of the Derbyshire receiver diminished in importance and in 1700 the post was abolished. Thereafter all the officials in charge of individual estates accounted to the steward in London, and those in charge of the Chatsworth and Hardwick collections handled local disbursements for the two houses and home farms.

Once this structure had been established, it was refined rather than fundamentally altered. The number of individual collections was reduced as areas were amalgamated, and in the late 19th century a Chesterfield office, from which the east Derbyshire collections were administered, was opened. As private country banks and later branches of the major London banks developed, receivers could deposit money locally, knowing that it would be transmitted the same day to the estate's London bankers.

Whereas in the 17th century the heads of the family had kept a personal eye on their officials, in the 18th century a senior official was appointed as auditor. It appears to have been the 6th duke who began to employ external auditors – his London solicitors, Currey & Co., who by the end of the century were exercising continuous oversight of a huge enterprise. Such use of solicitors was then quite normal: only in the 20th century, as taxation became more complex, did auditing great estates pass to chartered accountants.

What did not change, right up to 1926 when like other major landowners the 9th duke set up an estates company, was the ultimate object of the accounting system. The accounts were not intended to show whether the estate had made a 'profit' or 'loss' but to ensure that officials had received the money due to the estate and that their outgoings were justified. The family accounted with great care for everything they received and spent, which is one of the reasons why the estate survived so successfully for so long.

1670s and 1680s, in 1692 bought a mansion on the north side of
Piccadilly, with grounds running back to Berkeley Square, which
they renamed Devonshire House. This remained the London home
of the family until after the First World War.

At the same time the 1st duke rebuilt Chatsworth and
remodelled the grounds, and this became the family's principal
Derbyshire seat. The completion of the main period of rebuilding
at Chatsworth in 1694, at much the same time as the purchase of
Devonshire House, thus marked the end of an era which began
with the death of Bess in 1608 and the consolidation of the
Hardwick and Chatsworth estates in 1616.[23]

## Keeping the Books

Nothing survives, apart from one isolated rental of 1570, to
illustrate how James Hardwick administered his estates, and only
for the 1590s is much available for Bess's estates. Her accounts
show that she had a senior official, a receiver, at Hardwick to whom
the bailiffs in charge of each of her estates accounted, handing over
receipts from rent after making local payments. A second official
controlled outgoing payments and accounted to Bess. From at least
the 1590s and quite possibly earlier, although no records survive to
demonstrate this, her son William (Lord Cavendish from 1605 and
the earl of Devonshire from 1618) employed a system that differed
from his mother's in one important respect. Although he had no
London estate other than his own home, William spent part of
each year in the capital and, even when he was a widower living in
lodgings during the law terms and returning to Hardwick in the
vacation, kept a receiver in London as well as one in Derbyshire.
After William remarried in 1604, having shortly before bought a
house in Holborn, the London receiver's work began to expand. It
grew further as he bought estates south of the Trent and after 1608,
when he inherited other property in the Midlands and south from
Bess. During the same period the responsibilities of his Derbyshire
receiver increased through the same process of purchase and
inheritance, particularly after 1616 when William secured control
of his brother Henry's estate centred on Chatsworth. By the time
the 1st earl died in 1626 the two receivers were accounting for a
gross income from rents and other sources of around £16,000 a
year, and expenditure at about the same level.[24]

This arrangement of the family having two receivers, one
based in Derbyshire and the other in London, remained basically
unchanged for the rest of the 17th century. The only major
development, which seems to have been introduced by the 3rd
earl soon after he took charge of the estate in 1638, was the

emergence of the earl's steward as a third senior accounting officer. The 1st earl had a steward but he appears not to have been as important as his successors were; in the early 17th century most expenditure, as well as income, was handled by one of the two receivers. From the late 1630s, however, the London receiver (or, if the family were in the country, his Derbyshire counterpart) issued money 'on imprest' (i.e. an advance which had to be accounted for later) to the steward. Regular imprests were also made on a much smaller scale to the master of horse, who had charge of the earl's stables, and the keeper of the privy purse, who handled the earl's personal payments, and less regularly to other officials, including bailiffs of individual estates. Between the 1650s and 1670s, a period for which a lengthy run of accounts survive, most day-to-day household expenditure, including the payment of wages to servants, purchases of food, drink and furnishings, and travelling expenses for the family and their officials and servants, was being handled by the steward. Other regular purchases, such as clothing or books, which had been accounted for by the receivers in the 1st earl's time, were now paid for by the keeper of the privy purse. Both these officials, and the master of the horse, were peripatetic: they travelled with the family between London and the country and from house to house, whereas the receivers were resident at either the London house of the day or Hardwick. The growing importance of these travelling officials, together with the 1st duke's practice of living mainly in London, probably contributed to his decision to abolish the Derbyshire receivership in 1700.

Two consequences flowed from Hardwick's decline after 1700. One was that the Hall and its contents survived relatively unaltered until the 19th century, by which time their architectural and artistic importance could be appreciated anew; the other was that the muniments that had accumulated there since Bess's day remained largely untouched, apart from a few account books that were transferred to Chatsworth. Even though a vast quantity of subordinate financial records were obviously destroyed once they had been audited, the surviving books throw a wealth of light on how the Cavendish estate as a whole was run in the 17th century and how Hardwick itself functioned, both as a family residence and an administrative headquarters. They are particularly informative for two periods, the later years of the 1st earl's life (between about 1600 and his death in 1626), and the middle years of the 3rd's earl's time, between the late 1640s and the 1670s. There is much less on the 3rd earl's minority in the 1630s or the 1st duke's time, when most interest in the estate in Derbyshire is centred on the rebuilding of Chatsworth.[25]

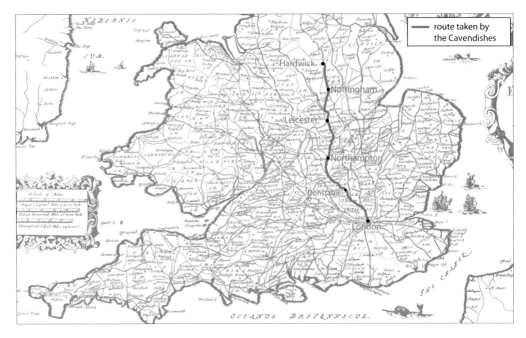

*Figure 35* The route
from Derbyshire to
London used by the
Cavendish family in the
17th century during their
removes, twice a year or
sometime more often,
between London and
the country. The journey
normally took five days
by coach, but about twice
that by waggon.

## LIFE IN A NOBLE HOUSEHOLD

What precisely life was like at Hardwick during the 17th century
depended on the circumstances of the family at any particular
time: whether the head of the family was single or married,
whether there were children at home, and how the family divided
their time between Hardwick and their other houses. Changes
in these circumstances would also affect the size and structure
of the household in personal attendance on the family, although
not particularly the staff running the estate. Even when the
3rd earl was in exile, between 1642 and 1645, small groups of
officials stayed at Hardwick and London to ensure that the estate
continued to function, if not as smoothly as before or after the
Civil War.

   As we have seen, an important aspect of the history of Hardwick
in the 17th century is that, apart from Bess in the last years of
her life, the family did not live there continuously. They were
not constantly on the move but they generally spent part of
each year in Derbyshire and part in London. This meant at least
two, and sometimes four, major journeys a year for family and
servants. From the 1st earl's time onwards the family had their
own coach, although when travelling alone male members of
the family may well have ridden alongside their senior officers,
and female family members also used litters (horseless carriages
carried by four footmen). The journey from Hardwick to London
generally took five days, with overnight stops at Nottingham,

Leicester, Northampton and one other place closer to London, most commonly Dunstable in Bedfordshire. Further north Market Harborough was an alternative staging post. The usual starting point for journeys from Hardwick, both north and south, was Rotherham Road, the main route across the limestone ridge that runs to the east of the house, which was more important then than it is today.

Both in the 1st earl's time and later the family travelled in some style, and their 'remove' from Hardwick, as officials termed it, was a significant event. Senior officials were given leaving presents, money was given to the poor waiting at the gates of the park, occasionally trumpeters played, presumably as the family left the house, and the party rarely travelled with fewer than a dozen horses. Their overnight stops, except at Leicester, where the family had a house, involved renting private lodgings for the family and putting the servants (and the coaches and horses) into an inn. Local musicians ('waits') provided entertainment and the church bells were rung in the family's honour. Money was given to the poor in each town: if the family travelled via Derby instead of Nottingham, gifts were made to the almspeople in the hospital founded by Bess. Particularly in the 1st earl's time, the removal of the Cavendish family from Hardwick to London, or their return to the country, must have seemed to the places through which they passed like a miniature version of a royal progress.

Some officials would have accompanied the family on these journeys but most servants travelled with the local carrier, whose journeys took about twice as long as the coach. Remarkably, some of the footmen appear to have walked between Derbyshire and either Latimers or London. Chesterfield already had a regular carrying service to London when the future 1st earl's accounts begin in 1597 and few weeks went by when his officials did not send something to London or receive goods brought down by the carrier. Mansfield appears also to have a regular service by this period, which the estate used nearly as often. In the 3rd earl's time Chesterfield had two London carriers, William Holland and Richard Marchant, and Mansfield one, William Hurst. Officials who wished to send goods up to London had only to take them a few miles to one town or the other; they did not have to go to Derby or Nottingham. One noticeable change during the 17th century is that whereas in the 1st earl's time the local carriers were clearly using packhorses, the 3rd earl's officials sent goods to and from London by waggon, although most goods moved between Hardwick and Chatsworth still went by packhorse. When the family went up to London in the 3rd earl's time, local resources

were supplemented by waggons hired from carriers based at
Spondon, just outside Derby.

Both before and after the General Post Office was established
in 1660, Chesterfield and Mansfield were also post towns, from
which a foot post (paid for by the estate) carried letters to and
from Hardwick twice a week. Sometimes letters came from
Higham, a village on the road to Derby a couple of miles nearer
Hardwick than Chesterfield. In the opposite direction, letters
were sometimes picked up on the Great North Road at Tuxford
in Nottinghamshire. By the 1690s, a decade for which a large
volume of letters written by the London receiver to his opposite
number at Hardwick survive, it is clear that letters in either
direction took only a few days to reach their destination and
rarely went astray.

The family generally did not send valuable plate by carrier.
When they shut up their London house for the summer they
handed over their plate to a City goldsmith for safekeeping,
withdrawing it when they returned in late autumn. Jewellery
presumably travelled with the family, along with items from their
wardrobe which they wore in both town and country.

Despite the complexity of the estate's accounting system, even
in the 1st earl's day, with rents coming in to two receivers from
estates hundreds of miles apart, and disbursements by officials
in Derbyshire and London, and by the family wherever they
happened to be, cash was only occasionally transferred in any
quantity to London. In 1602, some £14,670 had to be paid into
the Exchequer for a major land purchase from the Crown, and in
1608 about the same sum was sent up to London in two wains. In
general, right from the start of the 17th century, the Derbyshire
receiver used bills to return money to London. Throughout this
period about two thirds of the estate's total rent income was
payable to the Derbyshire receiver, but the London receiver was
responsible for the bulk of the family's expenditure, especially
towards the end of the 17th century, when the family lived much
more in town. The London receiver was also responsible for
supplying funds to the steward, the master of the horse and the
keeper of the privy purse, who only occasionally (when the family
were in Derbyshire for any length of time) drew funds from the
receiver there. As a result, the Derbyshire receiver had a surplus
every year of income over expenditure, which he remitted to his
London counterpart.

For a few years around 1600 the main agents used to return
money were Halifax and Wakefield clothiers. These were men
who travelled regularly to London, passing close to Hardwick
along the Rotherham road, to whom the Derbyshire receiver

*Figure 36*  The Royal
Exchange, the hub of
commercial life in the
late 17th-century City.
The earls' London
receivers came here to
obtain payment of bills
of exchange used to
remit money from their
Derbyshire counterparts.

handed over cash in return for a bill drawn on the clothiers'
London representatives, the Blackwell Hall factors. He then sent
the bill to the London receiver, who obtained cash from the
factors. After about 1610 this arrangement died out and instead
the receiver obtained bills from local men, almost all of whom
can be identified as Chesterfield lead merchants (although most
of them probably also dealt in imported iron and possibly other
goods). This identification is quite precise: officials did not go
to Derby or Wirksworth in search of lead merchants who could
return money, they dealt with men who lived in Chesterfield or
the surrounding countryside whom they would know personally
and expect to see at Chesterfield market every Saturday. The
fact that these men quite quickly supplanted the West Riding
clothiers as returners of money illustrates the rising importance
of the lead trade in the local economy in the first half of the
17th century, as does the size of operations revealed by the
1st earl's accounts. By the 1620s Chesterfield lead merchants
were returning several thousand pounds a year to London for
the estate, taking in cash and giving the receiver bills on their
London factors.[26]

Once established, this pattern remained largely unchanged until
the end of the 17th century, by which time the lead trade, much
of it still carried on through Chesterfield, was by far the most
important economic activity in Derbyshire after farming. Two
developments are apparent from the correspondence of the 1690s.
One is the increasing use of the bill of exchange, which could

circulate with endorsements to third parties instead of simply
being paid by the person on whom it was drawn, in place of the
simple bilateral bill used at an earlier date. The other is the practice
of the London receiver attending the Royal Exchange (or possibly
nearby coffee houses) to seek out drawees, rather than going to
their homes.

Although the evidence is less plentiful, the bailiffs of outlying
estates, both north and south of the Trent, seem usually to have
returned money to either the Derbyshire or London receiver by
bill, rather than carrying cash to Hardwick or up to town. Some
northern bailiffs actually found it easier to get a bill payable in the
capital rather than the country and so sent their rents direct to the
London receiver. The Keighley bailiff, for example, obtained bills
from local clothiers, who would have had no dealings in Derbyshire
and so their bills would not have have been known there, but who
would have had London factors.

The lead handled by Chesterfield merchants was carried
from Derbyshire to London by water via Bawtry and Hull, but
the Cavendish estate made limited use of this route to move
goods to and from London. Occasionally the London receiver
sent items this way, and there are also a few purchases by the
Derbyshire receiver of wine, salt and other goods at Hull in the
1st earl's time, which would probably then come by water as far
as Bawtry. A consignment of cheese, butter and bacon was sent
once a year in the 1610s from Hardwick to Bawtry, presumably
to be sent to London for the family's own consumption there.
Otherwise, it was the local carriers who were employed week
in, week out. In the first half of the 17th century, when the
Chesterfield and Mansfield carriers were using packhorses, the
usual rate was 1d. a pound, which rose to 1½d. after the Civil
War, an increase from 9s. 4d. to 14s. per hundredweight. By
the 1660s the carriers using waggons between Derbyshire and
London were charging no more than 8s. 6d. per hundredweight,
and by the late 1670s as little as 5s. 6d. The journey generally
took nine days, probably longer than by packhorse, but the cost
of carriage was lower.

## Household Goods

The range of items brought from London, and also the London
and Derbyshire receivers' accounts generally, illustrate both
the variety of goods bought by the family, especially in the
early 17th century for which the surviving sources are most
detailed, and the scope of retailing in Chesterfield, where the
estate made most local purchases. Both the 1st earl and his wife

bought their clothes and also furnishing fabrics in London, but children's clothes could be bought in Chesterfield. Some clothes for servants at Hardwick were also bought locally, although cloth of a particular colour for livery coats worn by London servants was obtained in the capital. Both adults' and children's shoes were bought in Chesterfield, where tanning was the most important manufacturing enterprise in the town and shoemaking a widespread local craft. Jewellery and gold and silver plate were always bought in London, although cheaper wooden and pewter tableware for Hardwick was obtained locally, as were all the building materials, including glass, timber, stone and lime (there is no evidence of the use of brick), needed for repairs there or the outlying houses at Oldcotes and Woodthorpe. Bar iron was also readily available: several purchases were made from the forge at Pleasley during the 1st earl's time, although there were other ironworks in the area. No specific references have been found to the purchase of cast-iron firebacks, although George Sitwell's furnace at Foxbrooke, near Eckington, was certainly making these in the 1660s.[27]

Both in the early and mid-17th century the foodstuffs most often brought down from London by carrier were dried and fresh fruit, including raisins, currants and figs, but above all oranges and lemons, which appear to have been unobtainable in local markets. Huge quantities were delivered, generally for 'my lady's use'. Both Elizabeth Wortley, the 1st earl's second wife, and Elizabeth Cecil, wife of the 3rd earl, appear to have been early believers in the value of citrus fruit in warding off illness. Some 'physic' was also brought from London for both ladies,

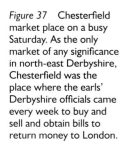

*Figure 37* Chesterfield market place on a busy Saturday. As the only market of any significance in north-east Derbyshire, Chesterfield was the place where the earls' Derbyshire officials came every week to buy and sell and obtain bills to return money to London.

although most medicine came from apothecaries connected with the family's doctors. In the country the 1st earl and his wife were attended by a doctor named Hunton who lived in Newark, while in the 1650s the 3rd earl used Dr Dakin of Derby. Both towns are about twenty miles from Hardwick. The family were attended by other practitioners when they were in London, including some of the best known figures of their day. As well as medicine, a wide range of herbs, spices and other exotic goods, including frankincense and myrrh, were brought from London for the use of the 'still woman', who was responsible for preparing preserves and perfumes for the family, both in London and the country. Expenditure of this sort reached a peak, much to the 3rd earl's annoyance, in the 1650s and early 1660s, when the still house was in the hands of Orlinda Mortimer, whose Christian name suggests that she was Portuguese and who seems to have favoured particularly extravagant concoctions.

Much of the food consumed daily by the household, and by the family when they were in residence, would have been produced on the demesne lands of the estate, which in the 1st earl's time included not only Hardwick itself but also Oldcotes and Woodthorpe a few miles to the north, both of which were sold during the period of retrenchment that followed the 2nd earl's death. But it is a myth to believe that an estate like Hardwick was self-sufficient. As well as imported fruit which could obviously not be grown locally, the estate had to buy in additional grain. Barley (or malt) was bought in large quantities from South Leverton in north Nottinghamshire, and also from Sutton in Ashfield, together with hops (which in this period were grown around Ollerton in central Nottinghamshire), to enable beer to be brewed at both Hardwick and Chatsworth. When the family were at Hardwick the baker went to Chesterfield market every Saturday, and to Mansfield most Thursdays, to buy 'fine wheat', which was presumably ground at Stainsby mill, to make white bread. When the family were at Chatsworth he went to Chesterfield and Bakewell markets. There were occasional visits to Alfreton market.

Meat would have been readily available from the home farms, although for a few years in the 1600s additional supplies were bought from Chesterfield butchers. Likewise, some fish would have come from the ponds created by damming the Doe Lea below the house. This source was evidently inadequate and, certainly in the 1st earl's time, when more fish may have been eaten than later in the 17th century, considerable quantities of freshwater fish, including eels, were brought from Stockwith, Gainsborough, Newark and elsewhere on the Trent, and from

# Coalmining in the Seventeenth Century

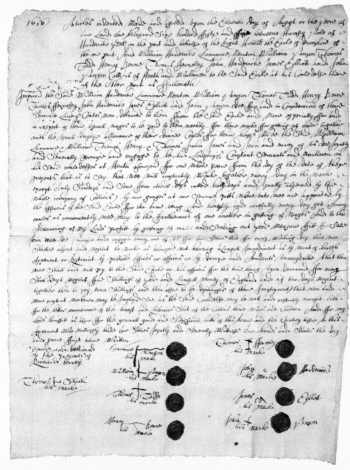

Figure A    *An agreement made in 1656 between the 3rd earl of Devonshire's receiver, Humphrey Poole, and nine colliers concerning the working of coal at Heath. The document is witnessed by Poole's assistant and successor, Richard Derrey, who was also licensee of the Hardwick Inn; the miners were unable to sign their names and so made crosses or other marks.*

Coal was mined on the Hardwick estate from Bess's time, if not before, until the mid-20th century. In the 16th and 17th centuries, the pits (often called 'delphs' by contemporaries) at Heath and Hardstoft were sometimes leased and sometimes worked directly by the estate. There are now no physical traces; pits have either disappeared with the passage of time or been swept away by later mining.

Early coalmining of this sort is rarely well documented, though references to pits appear in leases or rentals, and occasionally lists of tools in inventories. Thus the agreement of 1656 reproduced here, between the 3rd earl of Devonshire's Derbyshire receiver, Humphrey Poole, and a group of eight men who were to get coal at the pits at Heath, is a welcome survival which sets out how a small

mine was worked. The men were contracted to work as a team every day for a year. There were severe penalties for wilfully being absent, except on Sunday and the usual holidays, as it was deemed important that the pits were worked constantly for the benefit of the colliers' families, their employer, and 'for the general good and satisfaction both of this town and the country'. As well as their wages the colliers had been given livery coats (to indicate that they were servants, not tenants, of the earl) and were to receive 'dinnee coal' free for their own use. Both practices lasted until the end of mining in North Derbyshire: indeed, although NCB-liveried donkey jackets are no longer as widely worn as 30 years ago, many former Coal Board employees still receive a cash allowance in place of 'concessionary coal'.

*Figure 38* Stainsby
mill, an 18th-century
building on the site of the
medieval mill where the
tenants of the manor had
to grind their corn.

Thorne in the Don valley. Oysters came by the barrel load from
London.

In addition to the animals bred for their meat at Hardwick,
draught oxen used for ploughing were bought locally, but other
stock came from further afield. Estate officials regularly attended
the fairs at Chesterfield, Mansfield and Pleasley to buy beasts
for Hardwick, but also went to Lenton fair near Nottingham,
and into Yorkshire, both to Rotherham and as far as Pontefract,
Appletreewick (in upper Wharfedale, for sheep) and the Vale of
York (for cattle and oxen). The animals bought on these occasions
were driven back to Hardwick, or to one of the other estates
in Derbyshire or further south. In some months, especially in
the autumn, outdoor officials based at Hardwick travelled (on
horseback) considerable distances and were away from home for a
week at a time.

Particularly in the 3rd earl's time, when the family were securely
established as by far the most important landowners in Derbyshire,
food supplies were usefully supplemented by gifts from local gentry
and the larger tenants, who would send servants with meat or
poultry to either Hardwick or Chatsworth when the family were
resident. A regular gift from slightly further afield was apples and

other fruit from the tenant at Leicester, where the family's house was let after Countess Christian gave it up.

The other basic commodity available cheaply and locally was coal. It was mined throughout the 17th century (and later) at Hardstoft and Heath and, for part of the time, at a pit near the *Hardwick Inn*. Mining on the estate is well attested from James Hardwick's time, but there appear to be no references to earlier workings. This may simply be a function of the lack of surviving estate records before 1570. On the better documented Crown estate at Bolsover, only a few miles to the north, mining on the commons at Shuttlewood is recorded from the 14th century.[28]

On the Hardwick estate the pits were sometimes let and sometimes run directly by officials. Even when they were not in hand most of the coal was probably consumed at the Old and New Halls, which were assessed at a total of 114 hearths for the hearth taxes of the 1660s and 1670s. Until well into the 18th century leases on the Hardwick estate include a requirement for tenants to cart coal from the pits to the house. Some coal was presumably sold to tenants (there was no provision in leases for 'concessionary coal' in the modern sense) and possibly some was sold off the estate a short distance. It would not have gone far afield, since coal was equally readily available on other estates in adjoining parishes. In the 1670s (and one assumes at other times) coal was taken to Chatsworth: the cost rose from 4s. a load (i.e. the quantity a packhorse could carry in two panniers) at Hardwick for coal mined within a mile of the house to 7s. at Chatsworth, a journey of 12 or 15 miles, depending on the route taken. Coal was not taken to any of the family's other houses: in London the family, like everyone else, bought sea-coal from Newcastle or 'Scotch coal'. On at least one occasion in the 1st earl's time coal for Latimers was sent up the Thames from London to a wharf near Marlow; by contrast the 3rd earl's officials supplied Latimers with wainloads of coal sent by road.

The estate also made charcoal in Stainsby park, Langwith park and possibly elsewhere in the 17th century. Some of this may have been sold, but most would have been used at Hardwick for cooking, since charcoal is a much cleaner source of heat than coal. It could not have been burnt in the fireplaces, since these were far too big for anything except coal or firewood, which (as 'faggots') was produced in considerable quantities. Most of the timber needed for repairs and new building, whether at Hardwick, Oldcotes or elsewhere on the estate, would also have come from demesne woodland at Stainsby and Langwith. In addition, certainly in the 1st earl's time, small quantities of imported deal planks were bought at Bawtry or Gainsborough. The estate also occasionally bought 'Danske iron' at Bawtry, meaning iron imported from the Baltic via Hull.

## FAMILY AND HOUSEHOLD

How large was the household which waited on the family, ran
the demesne farms, and administered the estate as a whole?
Insofar as estimates can be made from lists of servants' wages
(which were paid twice a year, at Christmas and Midsummer), the
numbers seem surprisingly small, although some more menial
servants may have been paid through accounts that have not
survived. At the beginning of the 17th century (when Hardwick
was principally occupied by his mother) William Cavendish's
Derbyshire receiver headed a staff of around a dozen at Hardwick.
The figure increased after 1608 to about twenty, when some of
Bess's servants transferred to her son's household, although others
took the opportunity to retire on pensions left by Bess for William
to pay, including her main man of business, Timothy Pusey, who
was given £100 a year. The Derbyshire receiver's payroll roughly
doubled again in 1616, when he took over Chatsworth after Henry
Cavendish died. There were also about two dozen servants in the
London household, paid by the receiver there, in the early 17th
century, and about forty by the time the 1st earl died.

After the 3rd earl took over the estate, or at least after he
returned from exile in 1645, the number of servants remained
around forty but the vast majority were paid by the steward,
not the two receivers. Both Hardwick and Chatsworth, and the
London house, were left with only about half a dozen servants,
except when the family was in residence. An occasional residence
like Latimers had a housekeeper (in this period a male servant),
gardener and warrener, whereas Hardwick and Chatsworth, with
large home farms, had a husbandman or bailiff as well. All the
other servants formed part of the travelling household headed by
the steward, which contained the full range of indoor and outdoor
servants, of whom the cook was generally the most highly paid.
Other male servants included a coachman, postilion, footmen
and grooms. About three-quarters of the servants were men. The
female staff was headed by the still woman but otherwise consisted
of a number of maids, some of whom worked in the dairy and
laundry rather than the house. When there were young children
at home there were also women described as 'nurses'. In addition
to the earls' household, their wives had a smaller retinue of female
servants, whose wages were paid from the countesses' own 'pin
money'. Only one account book (kept by the steward of Countess
Elizabeth, the 3rd earl's wife, in the 1650s) survives to illustrate
how this other household functioned.[29]

At the top of each half-yearly list of servants were a handful of
officials given the title 'Mr', who were the equivalent of executive

*Figure 39* Thomas Hobbes, the greatest English political philosopher of his day, who joined the Cavendish household as the 2nd earl's tutor and stayed until he died in 1679. Some of the books he collected are still in the library at Chatsworth.

directors in a comparable business today. These included the two receivers, the steward, the master of the horse and the keeper of the privy purse, and also a domestic chaplain. All four earls had a clergyman in their household, who generally did not also hold one of the family livings in Derbyshire. Among the more interesting figures was a French Huguenot refugee of Genevan origin, Jean Saladine, who served the 1st earl for only a few years but was sufficiently well regarded to be given a pension of £30 a year when he left, which his widow continued to receive after his death.

Some of the chaplains may have helped to teach the children of the 1st earl, although tutors also appear on the wage lists in the early 17th century. Apart from the 1st earl, who attended Eton with his brother Charles for a short time in the early 1560s, none of the 17th-century heads of the family went away to school but were taught at home before travelling abroad with a tutor in their late teens. The future 2nd earl, whose education can be traced in more detail than that of later heads of the family, followed a conventional classical course of study, in which he was not joined by his sister, although she was certainly taught to read and write. Both had a dancing master. The family's most famous tutor in this period, Thomas Hobbes (1588-1679), drew a salary of £40 a year as the 2nd earl's tutor and later secretary, his son's tutor, and eventually simply as a pensioner whose stipend was a charge on the London receiver, rather than the steward, even though he generally travelled with the family. In the mid-17th century the future 1st duke's education, by a succession of tutors, was complete by the time detailed stewards' accounts become available, but there are payments to tutors and a dancing master for his sister Ann and his younger brother Charles. All the children appear to have been taught at least one musical instrument: the 1st duke's sister Ann played both the lute and guitar as a young woman.

## Family Life

Although the surviving accounts shed more light on the running of the estate at Hardwick than the daily life of the family there, the general impression is that throughout the 17th century the family lived quite quietly there, and presumably also at Chatsworth. Whereas in London the 1st earl and his wife attended the Court, and went to the theatre or to services at St Paul's, as well as visiting friends and relatives of similar social standing, there was less scope for this in Derbyshire. There was no commercial entertainment and fewer people they could call on. The 1st earl's personal payments include sums of a few shillings 'lost at play' (i.e. cards) but generally to his wife, rather than visitors. They also played

'Troulemadame', a popular indoor game in this period, not least among visitors to the baths at Buxton:

> If the weather be not agreeable to their expectation, they may
> have in the end of a bench eleven holes made, into the which
> to trowle pummets or bowls of lead, big, little, or mean, or
> also of copper, tin, wood, either violent or soft, after their own
> discretion, the pastime Troule in Madame is termed.[30]

Among the visitors to Hardwick in the 1st earl's time whose names are recorded are Francis Clifford, 4th earl of Cumberland, who stayed in March 1606 (when extra fish were bought for the occasion), and Sir William Cope, who came in September the same year, when Lord Cavendish lost 2s. 6d. at cards. Roger Manners, 5th earl of Rutland, the only other peer resident in the north of the county, with a seat at Haddon, visited Hardwick in August 1610, as did Henry Hastings, earl of Huntingdon, in September 1616.

When the family were at Hardwick for Christmas and New Year, small groups of musicians from neighbouring houses came over to entertain them (the Cavendishes themselves do not appear to have kept any musicians in this period), but there was no marked increase in expenditure on food and drink in these weeks, which suggests that the family were not entertaining on a large scale, as one might have expected. New Year gifts, certainly in the 1st earl's time, were confined to family members and small bonuses for senior members of the household. In September 1609, exceptionally, a company of actors (the Queen's Players) performed at Hardwick, for which they were paid 10s. In August 1614 a troupe of 'tumbling fiddlers' came to Hardwick at Lady Cavendish's command to entertain her young son John.

One reason for the lack of social contact between the Cavendishes and their neighbours was probably simply the gap that opened up between them in the early 17th century as William Cavendish was promoted first to a barony and then to an earldom. There were no other resident peers in north-east Derbyshire in the early 17th century, until the head of the Leeke family at Sutton became first Lord Deincourt (in 1624) and then earl of Scarsdale (in 1645), and Cavendish appears to have had little to do with either the 7th earl of Shrewsbury before his death in 1616 or his nephew, the future earl of Newcastle, who succeeded to the Welbeck and Bolsover estates when William's brother Charles died in 1617. Once he became a peer, Cavendish generally stopped going to Derby for quarter sessions or the assizes, instead sending senior officials to represent him, whereas in earlier years he had kept lodgings in the county town where he stayed for a week or two

*Figure 40* Staveley Hall, home of the Freschevilles until the last head of the family died in 1681, when the estate was bought by the 3rd earl of Devonshire. The Hall was later partly dismantled, but, with the expansion of coal mining, iron smelting and engineering in the parish, the estate became an important source of income for the Cavendishes.

when the circuit judges were sitting, presumably taking part in the social round that went with the occasion.

In the later 17th century both the 3rd earl and the 1st duke played some part in county life as lord lieutenant. After he resumed this office at the Restoration the 3rd earl gave dinners for 60 or 70 people at the *White Hart* in Derby or the *Angel* in Chesterfield when musters were held in the two towns, and the 1st duke's officials entertained in Derby during Parliamentary elections to protect the family's interest in both the county and borough seats, even though their master protested at the high cost afterwards.

By this period the gulf between the owners of Hardwick and Chatsworth and other local landowners was even more marked than it was in the 1st earl's time. Although, as we have seen, it was the custom for neighbouring gentry and the wealthier tenants to send servants with gifts of food to whichever of the Derbyshire houses the family were staying at, there is little evidence that the donors themselves were entertained at either Hardwick or Chatsworth. The era of a family like the Cavendishes throwing open their house to all who wished to visit them and hosting large meals with numerous guests was probably already largely past by the time the New Hall at Hardwick was finished in the 1590s. Certainly in the second half of the 17th century the family did more entertaining of this sort in London than in the country. The 3rd earl went on visits lasting a few weeks to neighbouring peerage and upper gentry families in Nottinghamshire in some years, but the only similar figure in Derbyshire with whom he seems to have had much social contact was John Frescheville of Staveley: the two went hawking together in the 1660s and 1670s when the earl was in Derbyshire during the summer. Both the 3rd earl and other members of the family also played tennis (i.e. real tennis, the indoor game) on the court built at the Old Hall at Hardwick.

The only royal visit to either Hardwick or Chatsworth in the 17th century occurred in 1619, when the Prince of Wales (the future Charles I) visited Hardwick; his father stayed in Derby. This was clearly a major event for both the family and the entire neighbourhood. Every landowner for miles around seems to have sent a gift of food or drink; the earl's sister-in-law Grace lent some 'carpets' (i.e. table-cloths) from Tutbury. Except on this occasion Derbyshire was probably just a little too far north to be included in royal progresses. When Charles I travelled from London to his coronation in Scotland he stayed on both the outward and return journeys at Welbeck, the home of the other branch of the Cavendish family, and made a brief visit to Bolsover, but did not call at Hardwick. This may have been simply because the 3rd earl was still under-age, although Countess Christian later entertained the king and queen at Devonshire House in London. A generation earlier the 1st earl travelled from Hardwick to wait on King James both at York, on his initial entry into England in 1603, and on at least one other occasion, when the king was at Nottingham in August 1614. In the later 17th century the family's contact with the royal family was entirely in London.

The overall impression is that, throughout the century, Hardwick was the main country home of a wealthy peerage family, occupied for some months each year but not continuously. When the family were in residence they were attended by a large number of servants, but when they were not Hardwick was essentially the administrative headquarters of a great estate, and also the centre of a large demesne farm, with the house itself kept clean and tidy by a handful of resident servants but probably with the main state rooms shut up.

## LIFE ON A GREAT ESTATE

The organisation of the Cavendish estate in the 1st earl's time is well documented, thanks mainly to his decision, taken about the time his mother died, to have his lands surveyed in detail by the mathematician and cartographer William Senior. Between about 1609 and just after the 1st earl's death, Senior produced a series of magnificent coloured maps of the estates, with an accompanying terrier, and did similar work for William's brother Charles on the Welbeck Abbey estate (for which the maps, but not the terriers, survive). Alongside Senior's surveys there is a useful run of rentals from the 1590s until just before the Civil War, although there is little evidence that either Countess Christian, the 3rd earl or the

1st duke commissioned a fresh survey of the estate as a whole. In the 1690s officials were apparently still using Senior's maps, even though for some manors they would have been badly out of date.[31]

Throughout the 17th century most farms on the Hardwick estate were let on 21-year leases. There is no sign of copyhold on any of the manors, either in Bess's day or later, and only limited evidence that leases were being granted for shorter terms by the end of the century or being replaced by tenancies at will. Cottages and smallholdings, on the other hand, were more likely to be let at will. Manor courts were still being held for both Stainsby (including Heath) and Langwith but were concerned with leet business rather than the transfer of holdings, and their importance would have diminished as the remaining open-field arable was enclosed. Throughout this period three obligations continued to be imposed on tenants: to cart coal from the pits at Heath and Hardstoft to the mansion at Hardwick when required, to keep a hound belonging to the earls' hunt, and to grind their corn at Stainsby mill. Other covenants in late 17th-century leases were conventional, such as a limit on what proportion of the land leased could be ploughed in any one year, and were intended to ensure good husbandry. The impression given by surviving leases is that the estate was administered efficiently but conservatively.

The main change that seems to have taken place is that the remaining open-field arable, which was still a prominent feature of all the manors around Hardwick in Senior's day, was enclosed. This process cannot be dated precisely, but at Langwith it had certainly been completed by the 1690s, and there is no reason to believe that it occurred any later on the rest of the Hardwick estate. A similar process of enclosure by agreement can occasionally be traced elsewhere, as at Beeley near Chatsworth, but in most places can only be inferred from the fact that all common arable had clearly disappeared well before the age of Parliamentary enclosure. All that remained to be done in the parishes around Hardwick in the late 18th century or early 19th was the enclosure of the remaining common pasture, as occurred at Langwith in 1748 and at Ault Hucknall and Heath in 1832, although the acreage dealt with then was smaller than that recorded in the early 17th century. In all the parishes in question, the Cavendishes either owned all the land or such a large proportion that enclosure of the arable could proceed without great formality.[32]

In the early 17th century each of the villages in the parishes of Ault Hucknall and Heath retained quite large remnants of their medieval three-field systems, as did Langwith. Overall about forty-five per cent of the land of each farm was open-field arable, although this average conceals figures as high as 80 per cent on

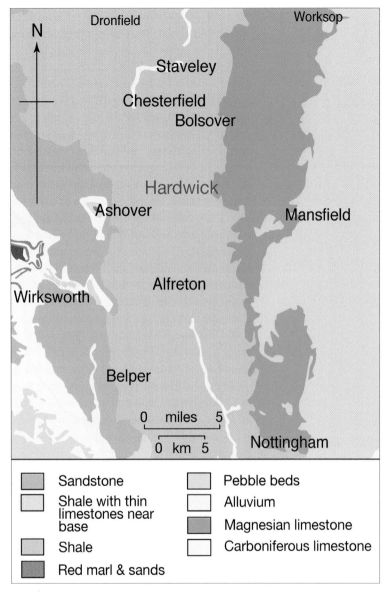

*Figure 41*  Geological map of the district around Hardwick.

some of the farms on the lighter soil of the magnesian limestone, as at Rowthorne. Some farmers may have had additional arable in the closes belonging to their holdings, for which Senior does not record land usage. The farms themselves obviously varied in size, around a median in Ault Hucknall parish of 47 acres; they would also have had access to grazing in the common pastures belonging to the manor of Stainsby and Heath. This average also hides a considerable range of farm size, from 11 acres to 128, although some of the smaller farms may have had land in neighbouring parishes. A good deal of reorganisation and consolidation had probably taken place in the period before Senior's surveys, whereas there appears to have been very little change for a long time afterwards. When Ault Hucknall was surveyed by the tithe commission in 1839 the median size of holding was 43 acres, extraordinarily close to the figure in 1609, and the proportion of arable was also virtually unchanged at about forty-three per cent. Enclosure, first of the open-field arable and later of the common pasture, may have changed the appearance of the landscape but did not greatly change the size of farm or the type of husbandry.

## A Picture of Farming

As in most communities in this period, the main source of information about farming practice on the estate comes from probate inventories. Those for Ault Hucknall and Heath tend to concentrate on the livestock on each farm, since they represented most of the value of the personal estate recorded in the inventory. In some cases the crops were dismissed merely as 'corn and hay', although in others more detail was given. The general picture deduced from inventories is that there was a more even balance between arable husbandry and stock rearing on the farms of the magnesian limestone which made up the bulk of the estate, compared with parishes further west which lay entirely on the coal measures. Here animal husbandry was more important.[33]

One of the most interesting inventories of those sampled for Ault Hucknall is that compiled after the death of William Hardwick of Stainsby in 1612. Hardwick (who may or may not have been distantly related to Bess – there is no evidence one way or the other) farmed 128 acres, together with a substantial holding in the common pasture of the manor. Only 10 acres lay in the open fields of Stainsby (Mill field, Brook field and Far field). Like all his neighbours and the demesne farm at Hardwick Hall, William used oxen for ploughing. Three were listed in his inventory, valued at £12 6s. 8d. out of a total personal estate of £85 15s. 8d. Hardwick also had 18 sheep and two bullock calves, presumably kept for rearing, as well as two milk cattle. Unusually, Hardwick's crops are enumerated in detail: he had wheat, rye, oats, barley and peas worth a total of £12 12s., far more than the figure in most other inventories for the parish of this period. The presence of all the grain crops and of peas, rather than beans, shows that even at Stainsby, which lies mostly on the coal measures, there was an element of light-land farming. Hardwick was growing barley, as well as the wheat, oats and rye characteristic of the coalfield. He (or his wife) was also producing wool from his sheep flock, although no figures are given for the number of spinning wheels or the weight of wool in his house.

*Figure 42* A rare
survival in north-east
Derbyshire, a cruck-
framed cottage at Heath,
probably built in the 16th
century. The cottage
was among the many
on the estate carefully
modernised during the
6th duke's campaign of
improvement. One of
the crucks forming the
original timber-framed
structure can be seen in
the end wall.

A similar picture of mixed farming, probably on the magnesian
limestone, emerges from the more modest inventory of William
Ludlam of 1570. He had four oxen for ploughing and two bullocks
for rearing, together with four milk cattle and 16 sheep, which
would have grazed on the commons. His crops are not named but
the corn and hay as a whole was valued at £6 12s. 4d., the second
most valuable item in the inventory. Ludlam was therefore engaged
in arable husbandry as well as stock-rearing, had a dairy herd and
kept sheep for their wool, and also had a few pigs and poultry. All
the other inventories examined confirm that oxen, rather than
horses, continued to be used for ploughing well into the 17th
century; all farmers of any size had a number of young beasts for
rearing and a modest flock of sheep. Corn growing represented a
smaller part of their activities: two inventories of 1567 and 1577
value hay and corn at £5 and £6 out of total personal estate in
both cases of about £35. On the other hand, inventories confirm
the picture shown by Senior's survey of arable farming alongside
animal husbandry.

What Senior's plans do not show, unlike some estate maps of
the same period, are realistic elevations of the farms and cottages
around Hardwick. A great deal of rebuilding and remodelling seems
to have taken place in the area in the 17th century (probably mainly
towards the end of this period) but the receivers' accounts do not
throw any light on this. Evidence from north-east Derbyshire as
a whole suggests that much of the replacement of timber-framed
houses with stone building took place quite late in the 17th century.

One cruck-framed cottage survives in Heath but otherwise all the older farms and cottages on the estate are built of local coal measures sandstone or magnesian limestone. There are no datestones *in situ* (a stone dated 1694 has been discovered out of context and re-installed on an unrelated building at Rowthorne) to help deduce when the process of renewal took place and many of the farms and cottages were extensively modernised, if not completely rebuilt, between the 1840s and 1860s. The only well documented house of this period on the estate is the *Hardwick Inn*, built in 1612, but this was much grander than most of the farms. Occasionally evidence of rebuilding can be found in wills: in 1587 David Sherbrooke, an Oxford-educated physician who lived at Northope Grange in Hardstoft, left the house to his wife, apart from the new parlour and two chambers over it, which his son was to have. Overall, it is difficult to say more than that in 1600 most of the tenants on the estate probably lived in timber-framed houses with thatched roofs of which virtually no trace survives, and by 1700 most of these had been replaced by stone-built houses roofed with local sandstone or possibly pantiles. A fair number of these houses, albeit much altered, can be seen in the villages around Hardwick today.[34]

WILLIAM 1st DVKE
OF DEVONSHIRE

# Chapter 4

# Hardwick and Chatsworth around 1700

*Figure 43* William Cavendish, 4th earl of Devonshire and (from 1694) 1st duke. The man who rebuilt Chatsworth and helped to topple James II from the throne.

Although in some respects the way of life of the first three earls of Devonshire and their families changed over the course of the 17th century, much remained the same between the later years of the 1st earl and the death of the 3rd earl in 1684. After 1616 there was no fundamental change in the size or shape of the family's estate or the houses available to them. Both the 1st and 3rd earls seem to have been mainly interested in managing their estates and neither played a leading role in public life nationally. They were important figures at Court and in Derbyshire, but that was merely a function of their wealth and standing as senior peers, not because they were office-holders. The most obvious difference between grandfather and grandson is that the 1st earl devoted most of his life to building up an estate, and therefore saw his rents increase year by year, whereas the 3rd earl had to devote most of his time to maintaining, rather than increasing, his income.

Underlying this continuity was an administrative structure developed by the 1st earl and adapted, but not fundamentally changed, by his son and grandson. One likely reason why it did not evolve much between the early 17th century and the death of the 3rd earl was that the family's estate (or other sources of income) did not change greatly in size or shape after the absorption of Henry Cavendish's lands and so there was no need to restructure the way in which was administered. Another was presumably that it worked well and neither the 1st earl, Countess Christian, nor the 3rd earl saw any need for change; the 2nd earl held the estate for such a short period that he would have had limited scope for making any changes, had he wished to.

The 3rd earl tended to complain about any sign of excessive expenditure he found in the accounts, or when figures in the Derbyshire and London receivers' books did not balance, but neither in his time, nor his grandfather's, is there any sign of dishonesty by officials. There were no dynasties of several generations of the same family serving as receivers, bailiffs or stewards on the Cavendish estate in the 17th century, although in a few cases sons followed fathers. Most senior officials stayed with the estate for a long time and those who did not die in service were generally pensioned when they retired, or given leases of farms on the estate. The earls were also generous in providing medical treatment for their servants, or nursing in their final illness, or in some cases, presumably when they died leaving no family or money, paying for funerals. There is no evidence from the surviving accounts or other records of anyone being dismissed in disgrace.[35]

There was also continuity in the administrative geography of the estate. The family lived in several houses in London during the 17th century before settling at Devonshire House in Piccadilly, but they always had a town house; in Derbyshire, Hardwick was seen as the more important of the two houses and the one where the northern receiver was usually based. In addition to overseeing the running of the home estate, the Derbyshire receiver was responsible for passing the accounts of the bailiffs of the other estates north of the Trent. There was some rearrangement of the bailiffs' responsibilities, especially in Nottinghamshire and Derbyshire, where the number of bailiffs was gradually reduced during the 17th century and the remaining officials given more estates to look after, but the basic scheme, with Hardwick as the administrative hub of the northern estates, was virtually the same at the 3rd earl's death in 1684 as it had been when his grandfather had died in 1626.

When the future 1st duke inherited this structure from his father in 1684 he appears initially to have made few changes, but by the 1690s the Derbyshire receivership was declining in importance. Not only did the duke spend most of his time in London, but expenditure which had previously been handled by the receiver at Hardwick concerned with the home estate was now being accounted for by the local bailiff. The receiver himself, James Whildon, had served the duke's father for many years and appears not to have adapted himself well to the new regime. The London receiver, Aaron Kinton, may have felt the same but was more tactful in his dealings with the duke, whom he saw much more frequently than Whildon did. Both men felt the duke should appoint what they called a 'riding steward', a senior outdoor official who would travel round the estates and keep a closer eye on the bailiffs than they could. Both lived to regret the advice. In 1700 the duke appointed William Grosvenor, previously of Newport in Shropshire, to take full charge of his estate. He was placed over Kinton in the London household, which he resented but accepted; more fundamentally Grosvenor evidently advised the duke to abolish the Derbyshire receivership and account for all income and expenditure in London. Thus Whildon lost his position as receiver after 23 years' service and was not replaced. He was kept on for a few years as auditor at Hardwick and his son John, who was the bailiff at Chatsworth and had been in charge throughout the rebuilding of the mansion, stayed with the duke for some years longer. James Whildon's retirement marked the end of an era which had lasted over a century. From 1700 the estate was run from London and officials in Derbyshire were based at Chatsworth rather than Hardwick.[36]

## CHATSWORTH HOUSE AND GARDENS

At the same time as Hardwick lost its position as an administrative centre it ceased to be the family's preferred Derbyshire home. The 1st duke appears never to have stayed at Hardwick for any length of time: in years in which his movements can be traced in detail, he seems to have begun his summer visit to Derbyshire, usually no earlier than July, by spending a couple of nights at Hardwick before moving to Chatsworth. There he received the local gentry and the officials in charge of his northern estates, before returning to London in October or early November. He does not appear particularly to have enjoyed his summers as head of Derbyshire society. In some years Kinton warned Whildon that the duke did not wish the local gentry to know of his impending arrival in the county and wanted to live as quietly as possible while he was at Chatsworth. There are also a number of letters from Kinton to Whildon suggesting that it was not always easy, as the summer arrived, to persuade the duke to leave town.

*Figure 44*  A panorama of Chatsworth from the south-west, in the 1690s. The mansion, rebuilt on the foundations of Bess's Elizabethan house, was surrounded by spectacular formal gardens, almost all trace of which was removed in the 18th and early 19th centuries to create the park landscape familiar to visitors today.

On the other hand, as soon as he succeeded his father, Devonshire started to modernise the gardens at Chatsworth. There are slight hints that the 3rd earl had begun to make changes in his final years, notably purchases of statuary in London which were probably for the garden at Chatsworth. It is possible that the 4th earl merely continued what his father had begun and accelerated the pace of

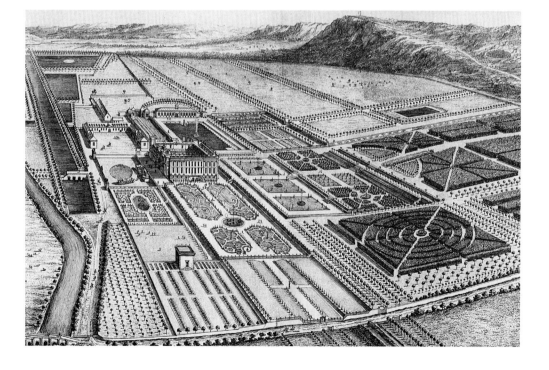

*Figure 45* The south front of the mansion at Chatsworth, designed in French-influenced style to resemble a palace by the fashionable architect William Talman who, two years later in 1689, became Comptroller of the King's Works.

change. Initially, the work appears to have been confined to some reordering of the gardens, which would have seemed rather old fashioned by the 1680s. The transformation of the mansion did not begin until 1688 when the earl ordered one of the four ranges of the quadrangular Elizabethan house to be taken down and rebuilt on the same foundations. Some years later, when the duke was in dispute with William Talman, the architect of the new house, and other contractors, James Whildon, possibly a slightly jaundiced witness, said that he had never been clear why Devonshire had decided to demolish one side of Chatsworth. As he pointed out, once one range had been rebuilt, the duke had little choice but to carry on and reconstruct the other three, involving him in far greater expense and trouble than perhaps he originally intended.

How much was spent can be estimated approximately from the Derbyshire receiver's accounts, although no record survives of purchases made by the London receiver. The main point is that Chatsworth was paid for out of current revenue, not savings or borrowings, which is an indication of how careful the 3rd earl had been in his management of the estate. Essentially the new house was funded by sharply reducing the proportion of Derbyshire receipts that were remitted to London. During the main period of rebuilding (1688-94) returns from Derbyshire to London averaged £1,420, compared with £3,840 in the years immediately before and after. In 1690-1 no money at all was sent to London, and the year before only £55. By contrast, issues to the official in charge of the rebuilding raised the total imprest on the Derbyshire receiver's account to an average of £5,745 in the same period, compared with £2,950 for the years either side. Local disbursements during the rebuilding also dropped slightly, from an average of £376 to £276. In round figures, rebuilding Chatsworth between 1688 and 1694 cost about £2,500 a year for six years, although the accounts show that some work was being done, particularly on the gardens, before 1688, and that other work continued after 1694. Since there was no reverse flow of remittances from the London receiver to his counterpart in Derbyshire, most if not all this money came from surplus income from the Derbyshire estates, including Hardwick, and the others in the north of England.

In the absence of the London receiver's accounts for this period it is impossible to say how much money was spent in London on the new house, either on craftsmen based in the capital who wished to be paid there or on furniture and other contents commissioned from London workshops. Nor can one see how the family adjusted to a drop in remittances from Derbyshire and thus in their disposable income. What is clear is that once the new house at Chatsworth was ready to be lived in, it became the family's main Derbyshire seat and, when the Derbyshire receiver retired a few years later, Hardwick Hall ceased to be the administrative centre of the estate. Thus ended an era which had begun almost a century earlier when the future 1st earl succeeded to the estates accumulated by his father and mother, and made her family's newly rebuilt home his main seat. Over four generations the Cavendishes had evolved from a slightly parvenu Jacobean magnate family into a dynasty of Whig princes. At the same time they had ceased to divide their time fairly evenly between a late Elizabethan prodigy house at Hardwick and a London house on the edge of the City, and instead had a mansion in the heart of the West End and a summer palace in the Peak.[37]

*Figure 46*  Devonshire House, Piccadilly, was built in 1734-7 on the site of Berkeley House to designs by William Kent and originally had a flight of stairs to a first-floor entrance. The house immediately became the duke's main home and remained the family's London residence until the First World War.

There appears to be no evidence, from the family's own
muniments or comments by contemporaries, to explain either why
the 4th earl chose to rebuild one of his two Derbyshire seats, or why
he chose Chatsworth in preference to Hardwick. Chatsworth was
the older house by about a generation. It would have looked old
fashioned and was possibly inconvenient as a place to live by the
1680s. But since, unusually for families of this status, Devonshire
had two great houses within a few miles of each other in the same
county, why did he simply not abandon the Elizabethan Chatsworth
and rebuild or extend Hardwick, which in earlier generations seems
to have been the family's preferred Derbyshire seat? It was the more
modern house and, until road improvements in the second half of
the 18th century made the Peak easier of access from the south, had
better links to Derby, Nottingham and London than Chatsworth.
Perhaps it was seen as too small or too difficult to extend, or
perhaps it was felt that a thoroughgoing scheme of modernisation
would have involved the demolition of both the Old Hall and
the New Hall, whereas at Chatsworth there was only one house
to deal with. There is also the point that as a house built round
a quadrangle Chatsworth could be demolished and rebuilt one
range at a time, leaving the other three sides (at least in principle)
habitable while the work was in progress. This would not have been
possible at Hardwick, although conceivably the family could have
lived in the Old Hall while the New Hall was being rebuilt.

Another possibility, which is perhaps suggested by Kip and
Knyff's well-known view of Chatsworth and its gardens, made
shortly after the completion of the rebuilding, is that there was
much more space to remodel the grounds on a grand scale than at
Hardwick. There the mansion stands on the edge of an escarpment,
with the ground falling away in front of the house, and a fairly
level plateau on the other three sides. It makes an impressive
picture from the west, although this view really only dates from the
opening of the motorway in the valley below in the 1960s. Until
then there was no clear view of Hardwick from a main road as one
approached the house from any direction. By contrast, Chatsworth
lies on the floor of quite a wide valley. To the east the ground rises
sharply to the gritstone edge of the East Moors, but to the north
and south the approach is reasonably level and one can see the
house from some distance, especially from the south. To the west
the ground rises gently to a low ridge separating the Derwent and
Wye valleys. But immediately around the house there is large area
of more or less flat ground in which there was more scope for the
kind of elaborate formal landscaping, with canals, terraces and
walks, fashionable at the time Chatsworth was rebuilt. There was
also plenty of water available from either the Derwent or streams

*Figure 47*   The interior
of Devonshire House was
designed as a magnificent
setting for entertaining.
The 6th Duke enriched
the decoration
but retained many
18th-century features and
the original furniture.

running off the moors to the east. Hardwick did not offer the same
scope for the kind of work that was undertaken in the grounds at
Chatsworth in the 1680s and 1690s. Nor would a new house on the
site of Hardwick have made such an impression on visitors from a
distance as Chatsworth did.

   One final point should be made about the timing of the
rebuilding: it was not undertaken to celebrate the 4th earl's
promotion to duke in 1694. Indeed, 1694 is traditionally seen as
the year in which the new house was completed, although finishing
works, followed by a lengthy dispute with the main contractors,
continued for some years afterwards. It is true that 1688, the year
in which work on the house began, is the one in which the earl
rose to national prominence for his part in the political revolution
that brought William of Orange to the throne, but he could hardly
have predicted at the time that six years later he would be rewarded
with a dukedom. Indeed, if the coup had failed, it is unlikely that

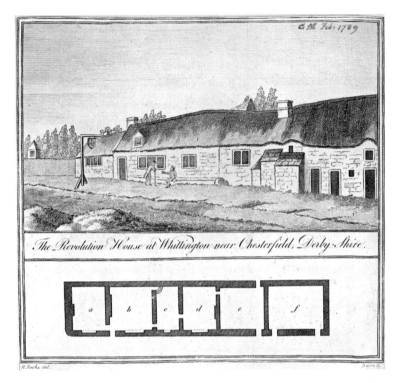

*Figure 48* The Revolution House at Whittington, traditionally identified as the alehouse in which the Glorious Revolution of 1688 was planned by the earl of Devonshire and others. Saved from demolition following the bicentenary celebrations in 1888 and since the 250th anniversary in 1938 maintained as a small museum by Chesterfield Borough Council.

Devonshire would have been in any position to rebuild Chatsworth in the years that followed. He had, after all, raised troops to march on Nottingham and Derby before James II had formally quit the throne and thus could have been accused of treason. It may be that both he and possibly his father felt that their great wealth, and unrivalled position in Derbyshire, meant that they should rebuild one of their country seats on a grander scale, but there is no contemporary evidence to support this notion. It is also possible that the 4th earl felt that his family's promotion in the peerage should have come earlier than it did: despite being on bad terms with his father, Devonshire insisted rather pointedly that he be given a funeral appropriate to a duke, not an earl. All this is speculation: what is clear from surviving family muniments is that the 1st duke had the resources to rebuild Chatsworth without burdening the estate with debt, which is a tribute to the skill of earlier heads of the family and their officials during several difficult decades.[38]

## HARDWICK REMODELLED

Hardwick was not entirely neglected during the 1st duke's time. It was during this period that the two first-floor suites of rooms on either side of the hall were remodelled and this work may have been supervised by William Talman, the architect of Chatsworth, who visited Hardwick at least three times in 1687-8. A little earlier, in 1685-6, some work had been done in the gardens at Hardwick, and during the rebuilding of Chatsworth some wainscot and other fittings from the old house there were sent over to Hardwick.[39]

The changes made by the 1st duke fundamentally altered Hardwick's position within the Cavendish estate as a whole. The Hall was significantly reduced in standing. The servants based there were simply responsible for the house and the home farm. The Hardwick 'collection', the lands traditionally managed by a bailiff based at the Hall, became one of a number looked after by a receiver (as the bailiffs had become known by the 1730s) who was responsible for most of the Derbyshire and Nottinghamshire estate. Nor were the manors around Hardwick of any special significance in the 18th century or the early 19th. Their relative importance diminished after the accession of the estates which had previously belonged to Richard Boyle, 3rd earl of Burlington, who died in 1753. Until then the former Hardwick family lands represented a larger proportion of the family's total possessions than they did afterwards. Even within Derbyshire, more interest attached in the 18th century to the Peak estate, because of the vastly increased income obtained in this period from its resources of lead and copper. This would change in the 19th century, with first the collapse of the mining industries of the Peak and then, a few decades later, the rise of the modern coal industry in north-east Derbyshire, but for a long period rents from the Hardwick estate formed only a small part of the family's total income, and a much smaller proportion than in the 17th century.

Hardwick never recovered its position as the main Derbyshire seat of the Cavendish family, nor its administrative importance. Except for a short period during the 5th duke's time, it would not again be used as a family home until the second half of the 19th century, and only towards the end of the century did it become an important source of income, thanks to the growth of coal mining. The changes made by the 1st duke around 1700 thus cast a long shadow over the history of both Hardwick Hall and the adjoining estate for the next century and a half.

# Chapter 5

# Georgian Hardwick

*Figure 49* The Old Hall was partly dismantled in the 18th century, but a few rooms continued to be occupied until the 1780s.

After his return from exile the 3rd earl of Devonshire divided his time in the country fairly evenly between Hardwick and Chatsworth. His son, by contrast, clearly had ambitions for Chatsworth as soon as he inherited the estate in 1684 and immediately began remodelling the gardens before starting on the rebuilding of the mansion. Once the new house was habitable, Chatsworth became his principal country seat and he appears to have used Hardwick only as a staging post in journeys between London and Chatsworth. In any case, to a far greater extent than his father, the 1st duke lived mainly in London. This pattern seems to have been maintained by the family throughout the 18th century, although direct evidence is limited. The sort of accounts that make it possible to reconstruct day-to-day life at both Hardwick and Chatsworth in the 17th century are largely lacking for the 18th century. On the other hand, for years in which the Hardwick bailiffs' accounts do survive, there is little to suggest that the family was in residence. No major building work was carried out at Hardwick, and indeed it was during the 18th century that the Old Hall began to fall into ruins. By contrast, extensive work was carried out at Chatsworth, notably the remodelling of the park and the building of a large block of stables to the north-east of the house.[40]

Hardwick, and the other Derbyshire collections which in the 17th century had formed the core of the estate, providing over 40 per cent of the family's total rent income, also declined in relative importance after the marriage in 1748 between the future 4th duke and Charlotte, daughter and heiress of Richard Boyle, 3rd earl of Burlington. When Burlington died in 1753, Charlotte, who herself died the following year, brought to her husband Lord Hartington, who succeeded to the dukedom in 1755, extensive lands in both England and Ireland. These included estates at Bolton Abbey and Londesborough in Yorkshire and Lismore in County Waterford, as well as the mansion at Chiswick and Burlington House in London itself. Of the family's older estates, those making up the Chatsworth collection remained important, not just because of Chatsworth itself but also because it was during the 18th century that income from minerals, including copper from Wetton and Ecton as well as lead from a number of manors in the Peak, increased greatly. The Hardwick collection, on the other hand, remained almost

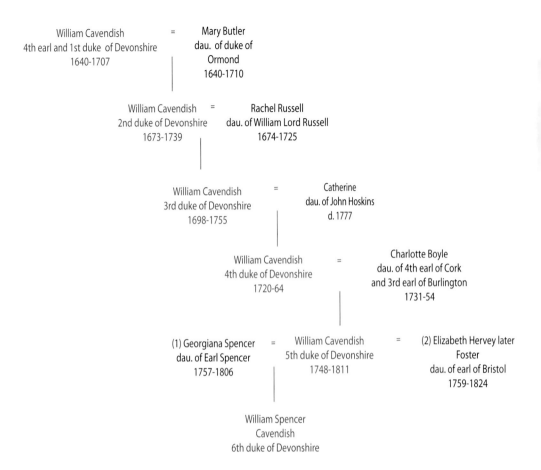

William Cavendish          =          Mary Butler
4th earl and 1st duke of Devonshire          dau. of duke of
1640-1707                                 Ormond
                                         1640-1710

William Cavendish     =     Rachel Russell
2nd duke of Devonshire          dau. of William Lord Russell
1673-1739                              1674-1725

William Cavendish          =          Catherine
3rd duke of Devonshire          dau. of John Hoskins
1698-1755                               d. 1777

William Cavendish          =          Charlotte Boyle
4th duke of Devonshire          dau. of 4th earl of Cork
1720-64                                 and 3rd earl of Burlington
                                         1731-54

(1) Georgiana Spencer     =     William Cavendish     =     (2) Elizabeth Hervey later
dau. of Earl Spencer          5th duke of Devonshire          Foster
1757-1806                          1748-1811                  dau. of earl of Bristol
                                                              1759-1824

William Spencer
Cavendish
6th duke of Devonshire

*Figure 50* Chart pedigree of the dukes of Devonshire, 1694-1858.

entirely agricultural, with only limited small-scale coal mining, until the building of the railways in the mid-19th century made it possible for much larger collieries to be sunk on or near the estate. The Georgian period, or the 'long 18th century' as it has come to be called, is a rather quiet period in the history of both the two mansions and the estate generally at Hardwick.[41]

## THE HARDWICK COLLECTION

Although Hardwick lost much of its administrative importance after 1700, the bailiff (or from the 1730s the receiver) based there continued to be responsible for a wider range of receipts and disbursements than his counterparts elsewhere, since he was in charge of one of the family's two main seats, including a large home farm. The structure established in 1700 proved remarkably durable, and the manors around Hardwick – essentially the

*Figure 51* The imposing front of the great quadrangle of stables built at Chatsworth by the 4th duke in 1758-63 to designs by James Paine.

group assembled by James Hardwick and bought by the future 1st earl of Devonshire in 1583 – remained a distinct administrative unit (a 'collection') until the office in Chesterfield, which dealt with all the Devonshire estates in north-east Derbyshire, closed in 1950.[42]

The first Hardwick receiver under the new regime was James Whildon's son John, who moved from Chatsworth once the main phase of building work there was complete. In the early 18th century income from the Hardwick collection was just under £2,000 a year. Most of this came from rent, although there was a small amount from wood sales. These included both mature timber and cordwood, cut from trees of about 25 years' growth, which was used to make charcoal. Most of the charcoal made on the estate was sold to the tenants of the dukes' ironworks at Staveley, which had been acquired from the Frescheville family with the rest of the manor in 1681. There were also small payments by farm and cottage tenants in lieu of actually undertaking the two remaining boons imposed in leases, hound-keeping and coal-carrying. Receipts from coal mining appear in the accounts only when the estate was working the small pits around Hardwick on their own account; in other years income from this source simply appears as rent.[43]

At the beginning of this period the dukes, like most great landowners, paid part of the land tax due on their tenants' holdings, in the belief that this was a temporary measure to meet the cost of William III's war against Louis XIV. When it became clear that the tax was permanent (in the event it survived until 1949) the concession was gradually withdrawn.

The chief outgoings to set against this income, apart from the receiver's own salary, were household expenses, mainly at Chatsworth, when the family was in residence, and local disbursements, mainly at Hardwick. These included, as well as the land tax rebate, the payment of rent on estates where the Cavendishes did not own the freehold, expenditure on the park and in the stables, and a small amount on household expenditure, implying that the family can have spent only a few days a year at Hardwick in this period. Once these payments had been met the balance of about £1,000 a year was remitted by bill to the duke's bank account in London, whereas before 1700 the money had been sent direct to the London receiver.

There were still no banks, in the modern sense, in the provinces in the early 18th century, and so bills continued to be drawn on Chesterfield lead merchants for payment by their London factors, as they had been before 1700, but there were now banks in

London at which families like the Cavendishes opened accounts. It is surely no coincidence that the first bankers in Chesterfield, the Wilkinson family, who were in business by the early 1780s, were also lead merchants.[44]

The early 18th-century accounts reveal a considerable contrast between income and expenditure within the Hardwick collection. If the land tax and window tax payments are deducted from the receiver's disbursements (since this money, like the remittances to the duke, ended up in London and was not returned to the local economy), and the household expenditure at Chatsworth is also disregarded, then on average the Hardwick receiver spent only about £450 a year on local goods and services. In other words, slightly under a quarter of the money raised from the estate found its way back into the local community, whereas just over half was paid to the duke and would have been spent mainly in London.

John Whildon retired as the Hardwick receiver in 1731 and was succeeded by William Barker, the first of two generations of his family who served the dukes, both of whom were based at Chatsworth rather than Hardwick. Under the elder Barker income from the Hardwick collection increased to around £2,100 a year in the 1730s, of which some £590 was disbursed locally, including about £100 on household expenses at Hardwick. This illustrates how the house was being run on a care and maintenance basis in these years. If the land tax is deducted from the disbursements, local expenditure falls to £540, about a quarter of the income from the collection. Thus the proportion remitted to London had risen to over 70 per cent.[45]

In the 1750s and 1760s, when Alexander Barker had charge not only of the Hardwick collection but also eight others in Derbyshire and adjoining counties, making him by far the estate's most important provincial official, receipts from the Hardwick group of estates, including cordwood and other minor sources of income, had risen to about £2,800 a year. As in earlier years the bulk of this money, on average about two thirds, was sent to the duke's London banker and most of the local disbursements were at Chatsworth, not Hardwick. The only remarkable item in the Hardwick payments in this period is one of £264 to 20 tenants in the collection (and others at Blackwell, near Alfreton, and the tenant at Unthank, near Holmesfield north of Chesterfield) after their properties were damaged by a hailstorm on 2 August 1765. During this period Barker made a rough calculation of the running costs of the two Derbyshire houses, suggesting that £2,000 a year was needed to keep Chatsworth going but only £400 for Hardwick: actual expenditure was often below these figures.[46]

*Figure 52* A tollhouse at Hardstoft on the Temple Normanton to Tibshelf turnpike of 1827, one of the few road schemes of the period to have much impact on the Hardwick estate.

## FARMING ON THE HARDWICK ESTATE

The 18th and early 19th centuries appear to have seen relatively little change in farming on the manors around Hardwick, in contrast to the period after 1840 and, it seems, the later 17th century, which probably saw the enclosure of the remaining common-field arable. All trace of the open fields had certainly disappeared by 1827, when an Act was obtained to enclose the last 300 acres of common waste in the parishes of Ault Hucknall and Heath (i.e. the manor of Stainsby). The award setting out the new enclosures was signed five years later. The area dealt with lay to the west of the villages of Heath and Stainsby, on either side of the road from Temple Normanton to Tibshelf. This road was itself turnpiked under another Act of 1827 and its course straightened where it ran over the former common. Two tollgates were built at junctions with minor roads near Hardstoft.[47]

Apart from this relatively late enclosure, there are few other signs of major reorganisation on the estate, such as the rebuilding of farmsteads or the building of new farms or cottages. Indeed, as we have seen in comparing William Senior's survey of 1609 with the tithe award of 1839, the number and size of holdings remained stable over a long period. The largest holding in 1839 was 181 acres and only eight farms out of a total of 41 had over a hundred acres. As usual with calculations of this sort, it is impossible to say whether farmers held additional land outside the parish in which their homestead lay, but the overall picture is clear. In the early

*Figure 53* A detail from P.P. Burdett's county map of 1767, showing the large area of common waste (Stainsby Common and Heath Common) which lay on either side of the Temple Normanton to Tibshelf turnpike near Hardstoft and Astwith until enclosure in the early 1830s.

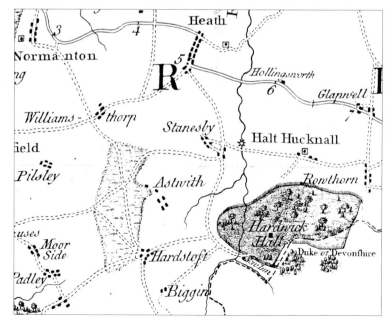

19th century, as in the early 17th, Ault Hucknall remained a parish
of generally small farms, and the largest were those on the lighter
soil of the magnesian limestone around Rowthorne.

There was also relatively little change in land usage. In the early
17th century about forty-five per cent of the land of each farm
in Ault Hucknall was cultivated as open-field arable; in 1839 the
proportion of arable in what had long been a fully enclosed parish
was 43 per cent. In the 1790s the most important crop on the coal
measures that made up the whole of the parish of Heath and the
western two-thirds of Ault Hucknall was oats. They accounted for
45 per cent of the arable acreage, compared with 33 per cent for
wheat and about eleven per cent each for barley and peas. On the
lighter soil of the limestone at Rowthorne and Glapwell barley was
more important, representing nearly a quarter of the total, and
oats slightly less so (40 per cent); as elsewhere in the two parishes
a third of the land was used for wheat. Peas were less frequently
grown on the limestone (four per cent of the total) and small
quantities of beans were also found in the district.[48] Writing about
ten years later, the Board of Agriculture reporter on Derbyshire,
John Farey, noted that 'A sort of round white Turnip, called
Stone-top, producing few leaves,' was being grown at Rowthorne
and elsewhere near Mansfield, and that swedes had recently been
introduced at Hardwick Park (when tried at Chatsworth it was
found that the hares and rabbits ate the plants).[49]

Thomas Martin, an official of the tithe commission who
surveyed the two parishes in 1838, found much the same picture as
40 years before. The coal measures produced a soil 'not of superior
quality', on which an irregular course of husbandry was pursued.
Most commonly, but not invariably, two crops of oats were taken
after one of wheat; barley was not mentioned in either parish
and clover only in Ault Hucknall. Even the magnesian limestone
at Rowthorne attracted only faint praise, Martin commenting
that 'the lime is a bad manure and good only for building'. This
echoed the view of the duke's agent, John Cottingham, about thirty
years earlier, that lime from Stony Houghton, when tried on the
Hardwick estate, 'has not occasioned the Seeds to stand, or the
Clover, &c. to last, so well, as when Crich Lime has been used'. The
Tithe Commission surveyor who visited Langwith in 1838, Edward
Greathed, described the soil as 'thin' ... Turnip and Barley land',
but the farming as 'very good'. Other crops grown were wheat,
clover and oats.[50]

One change that did take place over the course of the 18th century
was the gradual reduction in the length of leases granted to tenants
from the 21 years which was usual before 1700. This culminated in
the abolition of leases entirely on the Cavendish estates in Derbyshire

and their replacement by tenancies at will. This transformation was complete by 1800 and the example set by the largest landowner in the county was followed by most of the smaller estates. Farey criticised the change in principle, although it worked in practice on the Cavendish estate. The 6th duke, he declared, was considered one of the best landlords in Derbyshire, with the result that he had managed to secure the benefits which usually resulted from granting leases without having to offer more than yearly tenancies.

Farey marvelled at the improvements he saw on the various Cavendish estates in the county, all carried out at the tenants' expense: 'Houses and Premises Built, or completely Repaired, Fencing, Draining, Liming, Planting, &c., to the amount of some Thousands of Pounds on single Farms, and even Collieries effectually opened, on a good scale, by Tenants at Will!' Some of this may have taken place on the Hardwick estate (although Farey does not specify this) but, if so, it has left little or no mark on the ground and, as on most estates, no farm records survive from which it might be possible to trace expenditure by tenants, rather than their landlord. The only improvement which Farey observed being carried out by the duke's own officials on the Hardwick estate was some 'Shallow, or Surface-draining' on the coal measures to the west of Hardwick Hall'. Large-scale draining by the estate only began around 1840.[51]

Even for the home farm at Hardwick only fragmentary accounts survive for the 18th century. The most detailed are some cash books detailing disbursements in 1773-9 and 1784-99, kept by a man named Lexey Malinson, who appears to have been the farm bailiff at Hardwick. They show how small was the scale of expenditure at the house in this period, when it was clearly unused

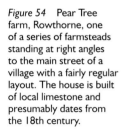

*Figure 54* Pear Tree farm, Rowthorne, one of a series of farmsteads standing at right angles to the main street of a village with a fairly regular layout. The house is built of local limestone and presumably dates from the 18th century.

for much of the time. In the year ending 31 December 1790, for example, Malinson received £835 from sales of farm produce and grazing, out of which he paid £668 in disbursements connected with the farm and £113 in servants' wages. After he had deducted his own salary (£50) there was a balance due to the duke of £4.[52]

Malinson may have accounted to Joseph Fletcher, whose accounts for 1785-93 summarise household expenditure at both Chatsworth and Hardwick in the same form as that found in Alexander Barker's accounts of the 1750s and 1760s. The charge (i.e. income) side of Fletcher's account included cash advances from the London receiver, John Heaton, via the duke's London bankers, Denne & Co.; sales of wood, including the value of wood delivered from Chatsworth to other places for the duke's use; sales from the garden at Chatsworth; sales from farming and grazing; and casual receipts. The discharge included expenditure on housekeeping (provisions, cellar, servants' wages and board wages, assistance in the house and offices, and sundries), the stables, liveries, taxes and assessments, preserving game, repairs to the mansion and offices, gardens and pleasure grounds, plantations, farming and grazing, gifts and charities, and sundries. In the year ending 31 December 1793 this expenditure, all at Chatsworth, totalled £6,621. By contrast, the disbursements at Hardwick, including repairs (£60), household expenses (£385) and sundries (£130), totalled £575, or about eight per cent of the total of £7,196 for the two houses together.[53]

## THE OLD AND NEW HALLS

The neglect into which the dukes allowed the two houses at Hardwick to fall in the 18th century can be exaggerated. The idea that the New Hall was left untouched while the Old Hall gradually became ruinous originates in Romantic ideas of the rediscovery of ancient mansions untouched by time since they were built, which became popular during the mid-19th-century reawakening of interest in the Tudors. Hardwick had particular appeal in this respect, given its associations with someone as famous as Bess (and also, quite fallaciously, Mary Queen of Scots). Hardwick was little used by the family but it was not deserted nor even, by the standards of the day, neglected.[54]

As we have seen, the 1st duke spent much less time in Derbyshire than his father and only stayed briefly at Hardwick, presumably to receive local gentry and the more important tenants from that collection. The 2nd duke similarly made occasional visits for short periods, when the small number of servants at the hall was augmented by 'helpers' who cleaned and aired the house

*Figure 55* An early 19th-century engraving of an imaginary scene of Mary Queen of Scots arriving at Hardwick Hall during her captivity in Derbyshire. The fact that Mary was never kept at – or even visited – Hardwick, where the New Hall was not started until four years after her execution, failed to deter Romantic artists from linking the exiled queen with one of the best known houses of Elizabethan England.

before the family came down and cleaned again when they left. Apart from some repairs in 1714 when a great wind toppled some chimneys and a carved coat of arms fell through the roof into the long gallery or New Hall, only routine maintenance was done at either house during this period.

This remained the pattern in the case of the New Hall during the 3rd duke's time, but was accompanied by the gradual demolition of the Old Hall. The building did not simply decay: portions were taken down and the materials sold at various dates between 1745 and 1767. The real tennis court was dismantled in 1751, presumably because no-one in the family was interested in the game any more. Under the 4th duke occasional visits were once again combined with routine maintenance.

*Figure 56* The Old Hall in ruins, as portrayed by a late 18th-century artist, when the house was beginning to attract attention from antiquaries.

*Figure 57*   Duchess
Georgiana, famous
for her connection
with Chatsworth and
Devonshire House,
appears to have been
very fond of Hardwick;
she and her husband,
the 5th duke, used the
house more than their
immediate predecessors.

The position changed after the 5th duke succeeded to the
title, aged 16, in 1764, and more especially after he married Lady
Georgiana Spencer in 1775. The couple made regular and quite
lengthy visits to Hardwick, usually of a few months at a time,
often arriving in October and staying until Christmas or later. The
duchess was said to be especially fond of the house, where some of
the old customs (presumably dating from the 3rd earl's time) were
revived. In 1774 prayers were said in the chapel for the first time for
many years and in 1797 a dance was held in the New Hall, an event
that had not occurred since the 3rd duke's day. It was evidently a
success and the experiment was repeated the following year. As a
result of this increased use the house was refurbished, with minor
repairs carried out each year between 1779 and 1787. The duke also
did more substantial work, including employing a plasterer named
Thomas Nicholls over a period of 20 years (1766-86).

A more systematic approach is evident from around 1785, when John Carr, the York architect who had been working for the Cavendishes at Chatsworth and elsewhere since the 1740s, began a seven-year commission at Hardwick. A total of £1,226 was spent between 1785 and 1791, although the work was so carefully done that its existence has only recently been appreciated. The roof was strengthened, new stonework carved for the rooftop and chimneys rebuilt. Floors and ceilings were strengthened and the plasterwork repaired in the long gallery, dining room, state room and great hall. The servants' rooms were improved: they were re-plastered and provided with new fireplaces, shelves, cupboards and doors. A new water closet was installed on the first floor.[55]

The house continued to be used by the duke and duchess after this work had been completed. They were resident at Hardwick between October 1797 and February 1798, and the following year the house was lent for a week to the newly married daughter and son-in-law of the Hunlokes of Wingerworth, with orders that the couple should be supplied 'with everything the place affords'. There were regular purchases of furniture for the house in the first decade of the 19th century, and a payment to W. & A. Dutton for playing at a dance in 1802. After Georgiana died in 1806 the duke used the house less; indeed, apart from one visit in 1809 there is little to suggest he ever returned to Hardwick.

The house was, however, the scene of a large party when the then Lord Hartington (who succeeded as 6th duke a few months later) came of age in 1811. This was a spectacular (and riotous) entertainment provided for the tenants and neighbours. Amid the drinking, fighting and confusion two men were accidentally killed, although this did not bring the party to an end. William Howitt, writing in the 1830s, saw events such as this as the personification of 'Old England' and Hardwick as a marvellous survival from a vanished age. But the New Hall only survived to achieve this recognition thanks to regular repair throughout the 17th and 18th centuries, combined with major works towards the end of this period; it was not an untouched Elizabethan gem.[56]

The growing, if not always very well informed, appreciation of Hardwick by early travel writers is well illustrated by John Byng's account of his visit in 1789: 'On a lofty hill crown'd with wood, and looking like a great, old castle of romance, stood seated, Hardwick Hall'. He admired the 'liberality of nature to this place', as evidenced by the boldness of its position, the growth of timber in the park, and the running water (the then unpolluted Doe Lea in the valley below), which was used to form what he called 'great pools', meaning the fishponds probably created by either James Hardwick or Bess. These he thought little of in their existing state but he considered that they 'might be made most superb'. When Byng visited he found 'many masons' at work in the hall and was pleased to find himself mistaken in believing the New Hall to be a deserted ruin, whereas in fact much work had been done in the last few years. He noted with disapproval that the duke was using deal for doors, skirtings and other woodwork, 'only fit for a farmhouse', presumably instead of English hardwood. It is in fact possible that what he saw was work on the servants' rooms. Byng also suggested spending £300 on carpets and grates: throughout its life Hardwick has been a cold house, even in the summer, as residents and visitors alike have discovered.

By contrast with the work done at the New Hall, the Old Hall was deliberately abandoned in the 5th duke's time and the remaining structure became unstable. Until 1789 the housekeeper, one of only three servants kept at Hardwick permanently, lived in rooms in the kitchen of the old building. She appears to have moved to the New Hall that year, after which it became completely ruinous. Byng noted that the Old Hall had been 'gutted for the advantage of Chatsworth' and was a sad skeleton when he saw it in 1789. The contents of the library created in the west wing for Thomas Hobbes in the 1650s had been removed to Chatsworth, where much of it remains today, but Byng did find himself 'amidst a large parcel of pamphlets, letters and accounts', including some addressed to Bess. These have since been lost or scattered, whereas the contents of the evidence house (or muniment room) in the New Hall, including much of the material that documents the family's history so fully in the 16th and 17th centuries, fortunately survived largely untouched, whether by damp, vermin or antiquaries, until the 6th duke had it catalogued in 1821.[57]

## PARISH LIFE

Although the Hardwick estate itself is less well documented in the 18th century than in the 17th, more information becomes available after 1700 about life in the parish generally, thanks to the improved survival of records at both local and county level. Local government around Hardwick was complicated, as elsewhere in Scarsdale hundred, by the survival of units that reflected the early medieval organisation of manors rather than parishes. The administrative geography of the area in the 18th century can only be properly understood by looking back to Domesday Book, if not before.[58]

In 1086 all the estates in the later parishes of Ault Hucknall and Heath were held by a leading supporter of William the Conqueror, Roger of Poitou. In 1102 Roger rebelled against

William II and his lands were forfeited to the Crown, including
what became known in the 12th century as the manor of Stainsby,
meaning the group of estates at Ault Hucknall and Heath.
Stainsby was granted out by Henry II in 1174 to the ancestor of
a family later named Savage, whose descendants remained lords
of the manor until 1593, when Stainsby was purchased by Bess of
Hardwick.

In the early 13th century two new estates were created within
the manor of Stainsby. One was Hardwick, held from the outset by
the family whose male line came to an end with the death of James
Hardwick in 1580 or 1581. Hardwick never acquired the status
of a separate manor, whereas the other estate, Rowthorne, which
was held until the Dissolution by Newstead abbey in Sherwood
Forest, did. In this way the parish of Ault Hucknall became divided
unequally between the larger manor of Stainsby, which included
the village of Stainsby itself, as well as Astwith, Hardstoft, Hardwick
and some smaller places which have disappeared, and the small
manor of Rowthorne, which comprised the village of Rowthorne
and the fields belonging to it.

To complicate matters further a second church was founded,
presumably in the 12th century, to serve the two villages of Lound
and Heath in the northern part of the manor of Stainsby; the
church at Ault Hucknall was already in existence in 1086. This
second church, at Lound, a deserted village which lay about a
quarter of a mile east of the village of Heath, where the burial
ground and some reused stone from the medieval church can still
be seen, acquired the status of a parish church. This meant that
Heath and Lound formed a parish separate from Ault Hucknall,
while remaining part of the manor of Stainsby.

Finally, parish boundaries strongly suggest that the village of
Glapwell once formed part of the area served by the church at
Ault Hucknall, and, at some date before 1066, may have belonged
to the same estate as the villages making up the later parishes of
Ault Hucknall and Heath. The modern civil parish of Glapwell
looks like an area that has been taken out of a larger unit, centred
on Ault Hucknall church, which would have had more regular
boundaries than the parish does today if it had once included both
Glapwell and Heath. In 1086 Glapwell formed part of William
Peverel's estate centred on Bolsover and remained part of Bolsover
parish until modern times, even though it was separated from
Bolsover by part of Scarcliffe parish. Presumably because it was
physically detached in this way, Glapwell remained a separate unit
for local administration, although for some purposes it was linked
with Rowthorne, which lies adjacent across the parish boundary
in Ault Hucknall.

Ault Hucknall Church and Parish

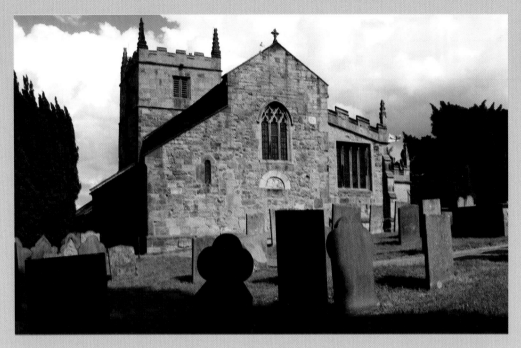

Figure A   *Ault Hucknall church from the south-west. The stonework of the 11th-century nave and aisle can be seen in the gable end. The blocked doorway and window are clearly part of the early building. The south aisle appears from its style to have been added in the early 16th century.*

In Ault Hucknall, as in most communities, the oldest surviving building is the parish church. St John's is unusual among Derbyshire churches in retaining features that date from the 11th century, probably from just after the Norman Conquest, when architecture was still influenced by Anglo-Saxon traditions.

The church has three compartments – a nave with a north aisle, a former chancel under a crossing tower, and a sanctuary (now the chancel). The chancel arch is small, narrow and pre-Conquest in character. In contrast, the arch opening from the nave into the crossing is decorated with 12th-century carvings designed to decorate an arch, which were probably part of the alterations made to the building at that time.

The external face of the west wall of the church shows that the nave and north aisle are part of the 11th-century building, as their original width can be traced in the stonework. The carvings on the narrow west doorway show Viking influence, but the small aisle window, with an arch formed of a single piece of stone in Anglo-Saxon fashion, is incised roughly with Norman zig-zag.

The fabric suggests an early foundation date, which is supported by the historical evidence. There was a priest on the manor of Stainsby in 1086 and in 1094 Roger of Poitou, the lord of Stainsby and several adjoining estates within the parish of Ault Hucknall, gave what he called the church of Stainsby to the abbey of Sées in Normandy, which his father, Roger of Montgomery, had founded half a century earlier. Since there is no evidence for a church at Stainsby itself, this gift must refer to St John's, which is named as Ault Hucknall church for the first time in the second half of the 12th century, when Henry II gave it to Newstead priory in Sherwood Forest. Roger of Poitou's lands were forfeit to the Crown in 1102, which may explain why Sées failed to retain the church.

The early date of Ault Hucknall church is also suggested by manor and parish boundaries. Until 19th-century revisions, parish boundaries changed little, if at all, over a long period. In many parts of the country, manor and parish boundaries coincided, but in north-east Derbyshire this tends not to be the case.

When Domesday Book was compiled in 1086 Roger of Poitou's estate included the whole of the later

parishes of Ault Hucknall and Heath, immediately to the north. If these two parishes are put together, the combined area is roughly L-shaped, as though a bite has been taken out in the north-eastern corner. The missing 'bite' is the township of Glapwell, which in 1086 was one of the manors held by William Peverel, the builder of the castle at Bolsover, his main estate in this part of Derbyshire. Because of this connection, Glapwell remained part of the ecclesiastical parish of Bolsover parish until modern times, although it was a separate manor and a separate poor-law township. If Glapwell is added to Heath and Ault Hucknall a unit with much more regular boundaries emerges, with St John's church, on its prominent hill-top site, standing close to the centre of an area that includes the villages, hamlets or farmsteads of Bramley, Glapwell, Rowthorne, Hardwick, Hardstoft, Astwith, Stainsby, Heath, Lound and Oldcotes

Speculation about pre-Conquest estate boundaries based on the evidence of later parish boundaries is often no more than that. In this case, however, architectural, topographical and tenurial evidence combine to suggest that St John's was established before the Norman Conquest to serve an estate of about 6,500 acres. Glapwell had already been separated from this unit by 1086, and in the 12th century a second church was built at Lound, which acquired the status of a parish church serving the northern part of what remained a single manor. Only the southern portion was left to form the parish that became known as Ault Hucknall, although it could equally well have been called Stainsby.

Figure B   *The carvings on the doorway possibly show the triumph of Christ's sacrifice (represented by the lamb and cross) over evil. The centaur-like animal on the semi-circular tympanum may be St Margaret emerging from the body of the Devil, and the figures on the lintel perhaps St George fighting the dragon.*

Figure C   *Nothing remains of Heath Old church, pulled down in 1852, except the ruined south porch and south doorway of the nave which has 12th-century chevron decoration. Two pieces of sculpture from the old church were placed in the porch of the new church. Both are 12th-century carved slabs of pinkish sandstone from the Hardwick quarries.*

Sources: Information on the fabric from R. Jewell, 'Ault Hucknall Derbyshire', 'Heath, Derbyshire' (1990) (unpublished), by kind permission of the Corpus of Romanesque Sculpture of Britain and Ireland.

This complicated manorial geography considerably influenced how local government developed in the area from the 16th century. During this period the official known as the constable, previously appointed by the manor, came to be regarded as a parish officer. In north-east Derbyshire, however, constables continued to be appointed for areas (known as either constableries or constablewicks) which reflected older manorial units. For this reason the parish of Ault Hucknall was divided into two constableries. One was generally known as Stainsby (but was sometimes called Heath) and included the greater part of the parish, together with the whole of the parish of Heath; the other was usually called 'Glapwell' but also included Rowthorne. At the same time, when the parish was made responsible by Parliament for poor relief and the maintenance of highways, the large parishes of northern counties like Derbyshire were often divided into smaller, more manageable units, usually known as townships, whose boundaries were in some cases coterminous with those of constableries. In both Heath and Ault Hucknall, however, the ecclesiastical parish formed a single township for both poor relief and highway administration. For these purposes, therefore, Rowthorne lost its identity; Glapwell, on the other hand, was treated as a separate township, quite distinct from the rest of Bolsover.

The administrative history of the parishes immediately to the east of Hardwick follows a slightly similar course. In 1086 the whole of the later parishes of Pleasley and Langwith formed an

*Figure 58* The small church at Langwith, drawn by Rawlins in 1823, serving another of the parishes on the Hardwick estate. Bess bought the advowson of Langwith in 1599.

estate named in Domesday Book as 'Houghton', represented on the modern map by the village of Stony Houghton. No church is mentioned in 1086 but two were founded in the 12th century, one at Langwith and the other at Pleasley, both of which became parish churches. No church was built at Stony Houghton, which remained a separate manor, part of which lay in Langwith parish and part in Pleasley. Langwith and Pleasley also emerged as separate manors, but in the 17th century the two parishes continued to form a single constablery. For poor relief and highway maintenance the administrative unit adopted was the parish and Stony Houghton lost any separate identity, although as late as the mid-19th century it was still sometimes called a 'township' and had known boundaries.[59]

## Work and Welfare

These complexities, which have been lost since the modernisation of local government began with the reform of the poor law in 1834, are important for several aspects the earlier history of the communities concerned. One of these concerns attempts to estimate their population before 1801, when the first Parliamentary census established the practice of using poor law townships as the unit within which figures were collected. The earliest systematic population data for Derbyshire parishes is a census carried out within each diocese of the southern province in 1563, which found that there were then 54 households in Ault Hucknall, 49 in Heath and 24 in Langwith. To obtain comparable figures from the hearth tax assessments of 1664, for which the petty constable was the local collector, one has to convert figures from constableries into estimates for parishes. For Ault Hucknall this produces a total of about a hundred households in the parish as a whole, of which probably 80 were in the portion in Stainsby constablery and the rest in Rowthorne. Heath had grown more slowly since the mid-16th century, and had perhaps 70 households in the 1660s; Langwith remained much smaller, with 28 households.

The returns to the other standard mid-17th-century source for population history, the Compton Census of 1676, include figures of 141 for Ault Hucknall and 70 for Langwith (there is no return for Heath). By comparison with the hearth tax data, both appear to refer to the number of adults, rather than either the total population (for which they are too low) or the number of families (for which they are too high). Three 18th-century sources – two archidiaconal visitation returns and a private census taken in 1783 – give reasonably consistent figures for Ault Hucknall (92 families in 1751, 70 in 1772 and 100 in 1783), suggesting that the population remained more or less static around a hundred houses or slightly fewer; the first census of 1801 returned a total of 97 houses occupied by 492 people. James Pilkington's census of 1783 provides the additional detail that, as well as the Old and New Hall at Hardwick, there were about 32 houses in Stainsby, 14 in Rowthorne, 28 in Astwith and 24 in Hardstoft. A similar picture of stability emerges for Heath, with estimates of 60 houses in 1772 and 64 in 1783, followed by a census return of 67 houses and a population of 378 in 1801. The same is true of Langwith, with returns of 19 families in 1751, 20 in 1772, 24 in 1783 and 31 (with a population of 156) in 1801.[60]

Although population data from before 1801 (or even in some cases the returns to the first census) can only be regarded as estimates, the figures for the three parishes which formed the core of the Hardwick estimate are reasonably plentiful and, perhaps more importantly, consistent one with another. The district was one which saw the population grow by at least 50 per cent between the mid-16th and the mid-17th centuries, before the rate of increase levelled off between then and the early 19th century. Like the other parishes on the magnesian limestone, including Bolsover, those around Hardwick did not see any precocious development of industry in the 18th century. Coal mining continued on a small scale but there were no workable deposits of ironstone. Nor did the parishes on the estate have much in the way of waterpower resources which might have encouraged the building of ironworks or early textile mills, as for example at Pleasley. They remained agricultural communities, with probably some framework knitting as a secondary occupation, although direct evidence is lacking. Writing in 1789 Pilkington noted that the population of Langwith was entirely dependent on agriculture, but he made no comment about employment in Heath or Ault Hucknall.[61]

Returning to the question of local taxation, contributions to the county militia were collected by constablery (not by parish or township) and these in turn were the basis of the general county rate levied by the justices of the peace meeting in quarter sessions. In both cases residents of Rowthorne could have found themselves paying more or less than their neighbours in the rest of Ault Hucknall parish, whereas all should in principle have paid the same parish poor rate and made the same contribution to the maintenance of local highways and also the church.

As surviving accounts illustrate, the parish was divided between the two overseers and the two churchwardens on lines that reflected the constablery boundaries. One overseer and one warden produced accounts for all the parish apart from Rowthorne, for which the other overseer and warden were responsible. The formula adopted was that Rowthorne represented one fifth of the area of the parish and both poor rates and church rates were apportioned on this basis, with Rowthorne finding 20 per cent of the total required. On the other hand, the poor themselves were

*Figure 60* Chesterfield Union workhouse, photographed *c.*1900.

not relieved strictly in accordance with this formula. Overall, the distribution of relief and the application of the laws of settlement, apprenticeship and bastardy seem to have been organised on a uniform basis over the whole parish. As a result there must have been occasions when one part of the parish subsidised the other from its share of the poor rate.

Both Ault Hucknall and most neighbouring parishes appear to have relied entirely on outdoor relief in this period, paying either cash doles or relief in kind to paupers who remained in their own homes. Of the parishes on the Hardwick estate, only Langwith subscribed to the local workhouse at Ashover. This was set up by a number of Scarsdale parishes who joined forces to use powers granted in an Act of Parliament of 1782 that foreshadowed the better known reform of 1834. The workhouse at Ashover was an early attempt to set up an institution that would provide indoor relief for the poor (more cheaply, it was hoped, than the cost per head of outdoor relief) and the only one of its kind in north-east Derbyshire before 1834, when a modern union workhouse was built in Chesterfield.[62]

The division of Ault Hucknall for rating purposes was made more explicit in the early 19th century, when one overseer was described as 'Overseer of the liberty of Stainsby' (i.e. the bulk of the parish, not merely the village of Stainsby alone) and the other as the 'Overseer of the liberty of Rowthorne'. It was not, however, a distinction accepted by the Poor Law Commission which reorganised the system under the Poor Law Amendment Act of 1834, when the whole of Ault Hucknall was treated as a single rating unit and placed in Mansfield poor law union. Conversely, Glapwell retained its autonomy from the rest of Bolsover and also joined Mansfield union, whereas Bolsover itself became part of Chesterfield union. Of the other parishes on the Hardwick estate, Heath was included in Chesterfield union, whose eastern boundary was generally marked by the river Doe Lea. Thus Langwith was put in Mansfield union, as was Blackwell, further south again. The unions created under the 1834 Act were supposed to be made up of all the parishes whose residents usually went to market in the town in which the workhouse was built (and thus ignored county boundaries). In fact, as we have seen, servants from Hardwick attended the markets at both Chesterfield and Mansfield in the 17th century and presumably continued to do so in later times. To some extent union boundaries simply reflected the need to create convenient administrative units.

Sixty years after the reform of 1834, when rural districts were set up, the boundaries of the new areas followed those of poor law unions but respected county boundaries. Mansfield union was therefore divided and Blackwell was chosen as the name for a small rural district made up of the Derbyshire parishes of the union, the rest of which lay in Nottinghamshire.

## Private Philanthropy

Alongside formal poor relief organised by the vestry, the earls of Devonshire, even when not resident at Hardwick, gave regularly to the poor throughout the 17th century. They also made frequent ad hoc payments to particular individuals, both young and old, or simply distributed money to the poor at the gates of Hardwick when they departed for London. Only in 1687 did the family establish an endowed charity to provide a regular income from which yearly payments on a similar scale could be made to the poor. The charity drew on two gifts, one made by Countess Christian in her will of 1674 and the other by the 3rd earl in 1683. The dowager countess left £420 to her son to buy land, the income from which was to be used to apprentice poor children in Derby or Edensor; the earl in his will set aside £400 for the benefit of the poor in Chatsworth, Edensor, Hardwick, Heath, Astwith, Houghton, Langwith, Hardstoft, Stainsby and Pentrich. Three years after the earl's death an estate worth £50 a year was bought at Rodsley and Hollington in south-west Derbyshire.[63]

In 1772 the vicar of Ault Hucknall, who was unsure how much of the income of the charity was received by his parish, reported that the money was given by himself and the churchwardens to poor housekeepers who received no weekly relief from the parish poor rate. By the 1820s, at any rate in Heath, Ault Hucknall and Langwith, the endowment had evolved into an apprenticing charity, paying premiums on behalf of young men and women whose parents had no money of their own.[64]

Compared with most rural parishes in north-east Derbyshire, quite early provision was made for a school on the Hardwick estate, presumably a reflection of the family's interest in their tenants. In 1724 a house on the northern edge of Hardwick park, about half a mile north of the Hall, was either built or adapted by the 2nd duke for use as a school. The southern part of the house dates from this period, with an eastern gable of fine ashlar and bevelled quoins, and a datestone of 1724. The house became known in Victorian times as The Grange; some adjoining woodland was still called School Wood in 1920.[65]

In 1729 Thomas Whitehead gave his house and 20 acres of land at Moorhaigh (in the parish of Mansfield), worth £8 a year, to his wife Dorothy for her life, which after her death would pass

to the churchwardens and overseers of the poor of Ault Hucknall
for them to hold in trust for the free school there. The rents and
profits, apart from 10s. for the purchase of books, were to be paid
to the master for instructing the poor children of the parish in
learning. This gift was augmented John Phillips, who in 1734 gave
£50 to the school, the interest to be paid to the master yearly. This
sum was placed in the hands of the 3rd duke and his successors,
who paid £2 10s. interest. In 1751, when the school was said
to have an income of £12 10s. a year, the children were taught
reading, writing, arithmetic and accounts, and instructed in the
principles of the Christian faith according to the doctrine of the
Church of England. By 1772 the school's total annual income
was £20, of which 10s. continued to be used to buy books. In the
1820s there were about two dozen boys and girls at the school
and the master's salary was £28 a year. The school still relied
mainly on rent from the farm at Moorhaigh, near Mansfield. The
master also received £2 10s. from John Phillips's charity. This
was less than the amount strictly due, but since the duke made 'a
considerable voluntary addition' to the master's salary the Charity
Commissioners felt that no action was necessary. The estate did
not establish schools in any of the other parishes in the Hardwick
collection until the 19th century.[66]

## CHURCH LIFE

The advowson of Ault Hucknall passed at the Dissolution from
Newstead abbey to Sir Francis Leeke. It was not acquired by the
Cavendish family until the break-up of the Sutton estate following
the death of the last earl of Scarsdale in 1736. The livings at Heath
and Langwith, on the other hand, were both purchased by Bess in
the 1590s.[67]

   None of the parishes had any chapels of ease in the early
modern period. In the Middle Ages both the manor house at
Stainsby and Hardwick Hall had domestic chapels. The first of
these would have disappeared when the house at Stainsby ceased
to be occupied and was demolished. At Hardwick it is impossible
to identify a room among the ruins of the Old Hall as a chapel,
although there may well have been one, as there was from the start
at the New Hall. This, however, would have been used purely by the
family and household for daily prayers. Otherwise all parishioners
would have been expected to attend services weekly at Ault
Hucknall church, which lay some distance from any of the villages
in the parish. In the parish of Heath, certainly by the early 17th
century and quite possibly for some time before, all the population
lived in the village of that name, rather than at Lound, where the

*Figure 61*
Newstead Abbey, a Premonstratensian house in Sherwood Forest to which the church at Ault Hucknall belonged for most of the Middle Ages. All that survives is the west wall of the church and the cloister which was converted into a mansion in the 16th century.

church stood, but nothing was done to resolve this anomaly until the mid-19th century. Only at Langwith was the church at the heart of the small village in which virtually all the population of the parish lived.

Ault Hucknall was not a wealthy living in the 18th century, since the bulk of the tithe income went to the dukes of Devonshire as impropriators (i.e. the successors of the medieval abbots of Newstead, who had appropriated the rectory), leaving the vicar with only the small tithes. Probably for this reason, the living was generally held in plurality, with one minister serving more than one parish. In 1751 the vicar was also incumbent of Scarcliffe, although he was resident at Ault Hucknall, where the parsonage house was described in 1698 as a building of three bays with two barns and 23 acres of glebe. In the mid-18th century services were held every Sunday and on four other days (30 January, 29 May, 11 June and Ash Wednesday). Communion was offered four times a year but at Easter 1751 only about a dozen received in a parish said to contain 92 families.

In 1772 the vicar, who held the living in plurality with Tibshelf, three miles away, where he lived, said that Ault Hucknall was worth about £45 a year. By contrast, the rector of Langwith, where the living had never been appropriated to a religious house, felt that a prudent man could make £100 a year, ministering to only about twenty families, although in 1772

*Figure 62* Samuel Pegge, antiquary and clerical pluralist, who numbered both Whittington and Heath among his cures. He was prominent, although by then in his eighties, in organising a spectacular centenary celebration of the Glorious Revolution in 1788.

the living was held in plurality with the slightly larger parish of Elmton, a few miles away to the north. Ault Hucknall then had one service every Sunday, whereas Langwith (where the minister was resident) had two; in both parishes communion was offered only four times a year. The third parish on the Hardwick estate, Heath, where the vicarage was worth £80 a year in 1772, was one of several then in the hands of Samuel Pegge, well known locally as both an antiquary and pluralist, who had installed a curate to whom he paid £30 a year. The curate in 1772 was John Bourne, the absentee vicar of South Wingfield, some miles away to the south, who lived at Spital House, just outside Chesterfield, and had in turn appointed a curate to do duty at South Wingfield. Like the other parishes, Heath had a service every Sunday and communion four times a year.

Church life appears to have continued at a low ebb into the early 19th century. Although in 1823 Ault Hucknall church was described as 'well attended', there were only 12 communicants and the building itself was dirty and in need of repair. The incumbent, who was also vicar of Heath, where he resided, dismissed the parsonage at Ault Hucknall as 'an indifferent thatched house', with three rooms downstairs and three bedrooms, 'not fit for a Clergyman'. Both the church and parsonage at Heath were in rather better order but still had only about fifteen communicants. The small but wealthy living at Langwith was then in the hands of Immanuel Halton of South Wingfield, and neither he nor his curate, who lived at Cuckney and was incumbent of two other Nottinghamshire parishes, was resident. The church was in good repair but the parsonage was a 'poor thatched house'. The 15 or 20 communicants would have represented a rather higher proportion of the population than the similar figures at Heath or Ault Hucknall.[68]

As far as one can tell from the existing fabric at Ault Hucknall and Langwith, or from early illustrations or parish records, no major alterations were carried out at either church in the 18th century. This lack of any new work adds to the picture inferred from replies to the archdeacons' visitations of incumbents and parish officers doing their duty in a rather passive way. Archdeacon Butler's severe criticism of the state of many of the churches he visited in 1823 did result in modest expenditure by the estate on those in which it had an interest. In 1824 small sums were spent on repairs at Ault Hucknall and Blackwell, where in both cases the duke received much of the income as impropriator. Blackwell was in fact completely rebuilt in 1827-8, when the estate spent £100 on the chancel and gave a similar sum towards the rest of the work. They also spent £25 on repairing the chancel and gave £100 towards re-pewing and other repairs at Ault Hucknall in 1827-30.[69]

There were small numbers of Dissenters on the Hardwick estate in the late 17th century, but support seems to have waned in the 18th century. In 1676 there were said to be nine nonconformists in Ault Hucknall (probably meaning nine adults, rather than nine households), and in 1682 there were six Quaker households in Stainsby constablery. In 1727 the home of Abraham Sampson in the constablery was licensed as a Quaker meeting-house, while in 1751 there were three families of Presbyterians and two of Quakers in Ault Hucknall parish, but

*Figure 63* Blackwell church was rebuilt in 1827-8, with a contribution by the Hardwick estate.

no meeting-house. Heath, for which no information is available for either 1676 or 1751, had no Dissenters in 1772; at Langwith a widow was said sometimes to attend the Independent meeting-house at Sutton in Ashfield.[70]

There were even fewer Roman Catholics in the parishes around Hardwick in the 17th and 18th centuries. Three people from Stainsby constablery were presented to quarter sessions in 1634 for not attending church, presumably because they were recusants; there were none in Ault Hucknall parish in 1676 or in Stainsby constablery in 1682; and in 1706 one was reported in Ault Hucknall (William Hall, described as 'journeyman to a clockmaker') and one in Heath (George Hobson, 'a poor servant, pauper'). The Cavendishes were quite strongly Protestant in the 16th century and therefore the area was not one where Catholics could hope to shelter behind the protection of a great house.[71]

# Victorian and Edwardian Hardwick

The 6th duke of Devonshire inherited one of the largest landed estates in the United Kingdom shortly after his 21st birthday in 1811. Between then and his death in 1858 he devoted great energy and a vast amount of money to its improvement, including major extensions to the mansion and alterations to the gardens and park at Chatsworth. From about 1840 he began a similar campaign of improvement at Hardwick, where, as we have seen, much less had been done in the 18th century than at Chatsworth. The changes affected both the Hall and the tenanted farms, although few new cottages were built. The 6th duke never married and at his death the title passed to a distant kinsman, who in 1868 conveyed the Hardwick estate to his eldest son, the marquess of Hartington, for his (the duke's) life. Hartington made some use of the Hall until he in turn succeeded as 8th duke in 1891, after which Hardwick was occupied only for a few weeks a year until 1938, when it became the home of the widow of the 9th duke.

The improvements carried out by the 6th duke, and continued on a reduced scale by his successors, did not lead to any great changes in the character of the villages around Hardwick, which remained almost entirely agricultural communities characterised by small, mixed farms. There was a good deal of rebuilding of farms in the mid-19th century but comparatively little new building, and only a modest growth of population. Similarly the Hall was modernised but not otherwise extended, and the park remained largely unaltered.

This stable landscape and society began to change after about 1870, when the growth of the modern coal industry began. Although the Cavendishes kept the collieries themselves out of site of their mansions and parks, they took full advantage of the expansion of the industry by leasing the coal beneath their estates. The sinking of the new collieries brought with it dramatic changes in both settlement and society on and near the Hardwick estate. New villages were built to house the miners and their families, and new churches, schools and chapels were built to serve these communities. The older, paternalistic society of a great estate was overlain (but not wholly obliterated) by these changes, and the dukes of Devonshire, like most other large landowners in the Derbyshire and Nottinghamshire coalfield, accepted that they owed

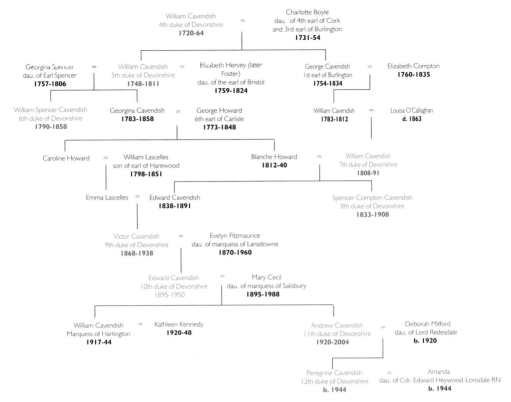

*Figure 65* Chart pedigree
showing the descent of
the dukedom from the
6th duke.

similar obligations to the people of the mining villages, as they did
towards the farmers and labourers in their older villages. The estate
thus adapted to the changes, benefited from them, and continued
to contribute to the well-being of the local community.

This chapter explores some of these themes, looking first at
the campaign of improvement carried through by the 6th duke,
on both the tenanted estate and at Hardwick Hall itself, and then
at other aspects of change in the local community, most of them
stemming from the impact of large-scale coal mining.

## THE MANAGEMENT OF THE ESTATE

In the early 19th century the Hardwick collection was let for
about £5,300 a year, more than double the figure for the mid-18th
century. There was a general increase in rents of around eighteen
per cent in 1829-30 which lifted the gross income to about £6,300 a
year, from which it rose gradually to just under £7,000 by the early
1850s. There was then a major increase of around twenty-eight
per cent in 1855-8, which took the gross figure above £9,000.
Steady increases continued in the 1860s and early 1870s, and in
1876-8 the rental was just over £10,000.[72]

On a national scale agriculture was severely depressed in the 1880s and 1890s and it is unfortunate that no accounts survive for this period. When figures become available again in 1892 the income from rent was about £13,000 a year. It increased slightly in the 1890s and 1900s to about £13,300 in 1912. The figure for 1917, under the somewhat artificial conditions of the First World War, was about £14,600.

In the early 1820s the accounts record only routine expenditure on repairs and renewals, together with occasional allowances to tenants who erected new buildings themselves. The first sign of more general 'improvement', which was to become a major feature of the Hardwick estate during the later years of the 6th duke's time, came in 1827-9, in connection with the enclosure of the last remaining common waste at Stainsby and Heath. Enclosure did not lead to major changes in farming in either Heath or Ault Hucknall, where all the open-field arable, and much of the common pasture, had been enclosed privately much earlier. A few new farms, of which the largest was High House on Timber Lane, were built on the new enclosures, but there was little amalgamation of farms or changes in husbandry. Ault Hucknall, in the mid-19th century as in the early 17th, remained a parish of generally small farms (the largest were those on the lighter soil of the magnesian limestone around Rowthorne). This remained the position up to the First World War. As J.J. Rowley summed up the position in 1868: 'The cultivation of the parish is mixed, but chiefly pastoral, the land of a medium quality.'[73]

*Figure 66*  Doe Lea colliery, known locally as 'Dominic's' since it was established and for many years run by Dominic Lavin. The small scale of the surface buildings and the lack of any railway connection evident here were typical of licensed mines throughout the British coalfield, and are in marked contrast with Hardwick and Williamthorpe collieries nearby.

*Figure 67* The *Devonshire Arms* at Upper Langwith, which was largely rebuilt by the estate *c.*1840.

The picture obtained from the estate accounts is reinforced by the figures collected annually from farmers in each parish from 1866 by the Board of Agriculture. These show that the structure of farming in Ault Hucknall remained remarkably stable in the second half of the 19th century and beyond, which must reflect a policy of consistent, if conservative, management. The lack of change in the number and size of farms recorded in the official statistics between 1870 and 1930 suggest no more than a small amount of consolidation here and there. There were 41 farms of 10 acres or over in 1838, when tithes were commuted, and exactly the same figure a century later in 1941. In 1910 there were 30 farms of 20 acres or more, and 25 smallholdings with between two and 18 acres.

There was also relatively little change in land usage. In the late 1830s about forty-three per cent of the land of each farm was ploughed. Arable farming remained of considerable importance in Ault Hucknall until the Great Depression of the 1880s, when much of the land was laid down to permanent pasture, as farmers moved more towards livestock raising. The First and Second World Wars, with their emphasis on maximising food production, led to a revival of arable farming. The net result in Ault Hucknall was that the division between arable and grass in 1941, under wartime conditions, was very similar to that in 1839, when arable farming also predominated. On the other hand, the cropping figures for 1870, 1900 and 1930 indicate a smaller area under the plough than at either end of the period. Despite these changes, the basic principles of farming on the estate remained the same and continued to reflect the mixture of light and heavy land. The wheat and barley of the clays, with substantial herds of cattle, operated side by side with the barley, roots and temporary grasses, with their attendant sheep flocks, on the lighter side. Mangolds, the root fodder crop of the clays, were cultivated alongside the turnips and swedes of the lighter soils. Overall, it was a balanced, mixed economy, with most of the larger farms involved in stock rearing, milk, cash crops, fodder crops and various minor enterprises, such as poultry, and a small amount of fruit farming.

Livestock numbers changed slightly over the period: although cattle, kept for both milk and beef, were always more important than sheep, the difference increased in the first half of the 20th century, by which time only a few farms had large sheep flocks. Most farms kept some pigs, but specialist pig farms were not a characteristic of the district.[74]

## Farm Buildings

Whilst farm size and farming practice did not change during the 6th duke's time (or indeed before and after), other improvements were afoot in this period. By 1840 the Hardwick receiver was beginning to erect new farm buildings on the estate, and in 1839-41 spent £470 on rebuilding the *Devonshire Arms* public house at Upper Langwith. Throughout the 1840s and early 1850s the rebuilding campaign gathered momentum. Expenses set against the Hardwick rental, which had averaged about £130 a year between 1818 and 1835, increased to around £740 a year over the

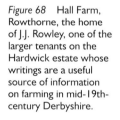

*Figure 68* Hall Farm, Rowthorne, the home of J.J. Rowley, one of the larger tenants on the Hardwick estate whose writings are a useful source of information on farming in mid-19th-century Derbyshire.

following decade, before rising again between 1845 and 1858, a period in which the average was £3,900 a year. Expenditure peaked at about £6,500 in 1858, the year of the 6th duke's death.

Most (although not all) of this increase was the result of a major renewal of farmhouses, farm buildings and cottages throughout the Hardwick estate, combined with some new building. In some cases the farmhouse appears to have been entirely taken down and rebuilt, and in others the level of expenditure suggests that completely new sets of buildings were erected. Over the estate as a whole, especially in Ault Hucknall and Heath, where in both cases the duke owned almost all the parish, there must have been more rebuilding in the 15 years up to 1858 than at any time for at least a century and probably much longer.

A close study of the 10 largest farms in Ault Hucknall (including Biggin, which lies just inside Tibshelf parish) shows that the pattern of improvement was similar on each of the holdings. Farmhouses were extensively modernised, and in some cases entirely rebuilt. The most common walling material remained stone, although bricks from an estate brickyard at Hardstoft were also used. Slate or pantile replaced thatch on the roofs. In at least one case, Stainsby Farm, a marble chimneypiece was installed as part of the improvements. One tenant, John Jepson Rowley, in 1844 extended and improved Hall Farm at Rowthorne at his own expense. Rowley stands slightly apart from his fellow tenants, as does Hall Farm, which has a rather grander appearance than most of the farms on the estate. He was the author of the essay on Derbyshire in the series on each county published by the Royal Agricultural Society in 1853, exhibited a piece of agricultural machinery of his own design at the Great Exhibition in 1851, and in 1868 gave evidence to the commission investigating the employment of women and children in agriculture. Despite these improvements, a further £900 was spent on the farm by the estate in 1873-5 after a new tenant succeeded Rowley.

Where farm buildings were replaced the usual layout was quadrangular, in accordance with textbook recommendations of the period. A complete rebuilding from the foundations up seems to have cost around £900 on a large farm, such as Hucknall Farm (next to Ault Hucknall church) or Stainsby Farm. The holding on which most was spent in this period was the *Hardwick Inn*, which in this period was both a pub and a farm. The house itself was extensively modernised in 1852 at a cost of £949. The works included a detached 'pavilion' at the rear. This has since disappeared but probably stood on the site of the present dining room, itself a 20th-century addition to the building. The other rooms were reorganised to create more or less the layout seen by the visitor today. Between 1857 and 1860 a further £1,466 was

*Figure 69* One of the cottages at Heath modernised by the 6th duke and probably made to look more 17th-century than it did before.

spent on a new set of farm buildings to the west of the inn, which formed a quadrangle with an ornamental frontage on the side facing the pub entrance. This level of expenditure and the quality of the work presumably reflect the position of the *Hardwick Inn* at the main entrance to the park.[75]

## Estate Improvements

As well as the improvements to the farms, a good deal of work was also done at Stainsby mill in this period, including the installation of new machinery costing over £500 in 1849-50. What the estate did not do, on the other hand, was build enough new cottages. Rowley noted in 1868 that there was a scarcity of accommodation for labourers in the district: 'a rural population has not been encouraged, and a scarcity of hands in a busy season is the result'. Very few new cottages had been built in Ault Hucknall, and the older houses were not conveniently situated, which meant that labourers had to walk several miles to and from work. The cottages had good gardens but no allotments had been provided.[76]

No architect is named in the accounts as being responsible for the campaign of modernisation, although work undertaken during the same period at Hardwick Hall was supervised by Samuel Rollinson of Chesterfield and he may have played some

*Figure 70* A plan of the farm buildings at High House, Timber Lane, laid out in a quadrangle according to the best textbook advice of the period. An example of the 6th duke's improvements to farms on the estate in the 1840s and 1850s.

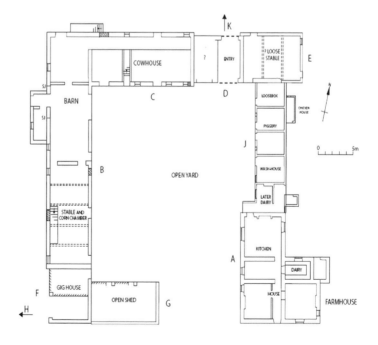

*Figure 71*  Some of
the solidly constructed
stone buildings at
High House farm.

part in the rebuilding of the farms. In general the work was done
in a conservative style, without any standard design or 'master
plan'. There are no 'model farms' in the conventional sense on the
Hardwick estate, which elsewhere stand out from older buildings.
Farmhouses were enlarged and buildings rearranged on more
modern lines around a paved yard, but materials remained
traditional. The detailing of doors and windows in some cases
appears to be self-consciously antique, so that some buildings
on the estate, such as the *Hardwick Inn* and Stainsby mill,
probably looked more 17th-century in character after rebuilding
than before.

   At the same time as undertaking a great deal of rebuilding,
the estate also carried out an extensive programme of draining.
In 1849-50 the receiver obtained 25 copies of a pamphlet on
the advantages of under-draining, presumably to give to the
principal tenants in his collection, and spent £167 on draining
several farms that year. Similar payments are recorded in each
of the remaining years of the 6th duke's life, averaging £250
between 1849 and 1858. This excludes the cost of tiles and
other materials, and also other expenditure, such as fencing and
walling, which was later included under the heading of 'draining
and improvements'.

   As well as buying the pamphlets, the duke also that year
engaged James Haywood of Sheffield to give five lectures to
Heath Farmers' Club. The club appears to have been a short-lived
venture whose (presumably recent) establishment implies that
the estate was trying to encourage a spirit of improvement among

the tenants. Other similar payments include a subscription to the North Derbyshire Agricultural Society from 1836, and in 1847 several estate employees had their fares paid to attend a meeting of the Royal Agricultural Society at York. From 1856 the estate subscribed to Clay Cross Horticultural Society (a parish in which it had few interests) and from 1861 to Tibshelf Agricultural Club. From 1875 the Hucknall under Huthwaite Floral and Horticultural Society also received a guinea a year, as did a similar body in Tibshelf in 1877.

Neither rebuilding nor other improvements stopped at the duke's death: between 1860 and 1868 estate expenses, still largely driven by these two budget heads, averaged just over £4,000 a year.

*Figure 72* Plan of Stainsby mill, showing the layout in the 19th century.

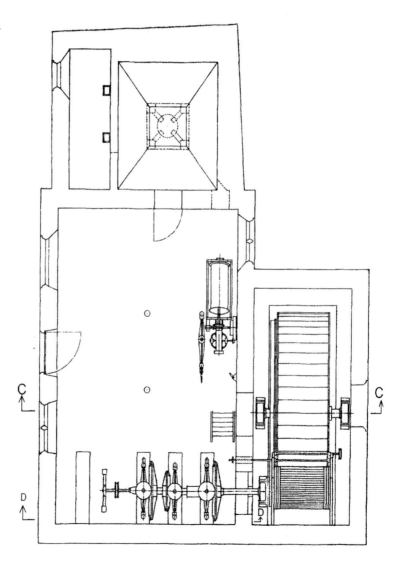

In the case of building work, it is difficult to distinguish routine repairs and renewals from major reconstruction or rebuilding, but under 'draining and improvement' an average of £780 was spent each year between 1858 and 1868. Expenditure fell during the first decade in which Lord Hartington was responsible for Hardwick, to an annual average of £2,900 between 1868 and 1878, of which draining and other improvements accounted for an average of £490 a year. In 1871-2 the waterwheel and gears at Stainsby mill were replaced at a cost of £221.

For the period after 1892 repairs are clearly separated from new building, and 'draining and improvement' continued to be used as a budget head, although between then and 1917 expenditure averaged only about £30 a year. Similarly, new building accounted for only £275 a year, whereas repairs amounted to £1,700 a year.

## A Farming Community

The improvements carried out during both during the 6th duke's time and later did not lead to any significant change in the pattern of settlement on the estate, any more than enclosure had done in the 1820s. Nor, as Rowley noted, was there much increase in the number of cottages. The population of Ault Hucknall parish rose steadily from 492 in 1801 to a peak of 690 in 1851, before falling back to 639 after 20 years. It only started to increase with the building of cottages (at what became the village named Doe Lea) to house miners working at Glapwell colliery, where sinking began in 1882. The population of Heath was 378 in both 1801 and 1851 (with modest changes between those dates), and was still only 403 in 1891, a few years before the village of Holmewood was built, again to serve two nearby collieries, Hardwick and Williamthorpe. Langwith was smaller still, with fewer than 200 people in every census down to 1871, before a slight increase began.

Before the growth of mining, Ault Hucknall and neighbouring parishes were almost entirely agricultural. Once again, J.J. Rowley provides the best picture of what life was like for most of the population. In the 1860s adult male farm labourers worked from 6.30 a.m. to 5 p.m. in the summer, with 1½ hours at midday for 'bait'. In the winter they worked from 8 a.m. to 4 p.m. without a break. Boys aged from nine to 12 were employed to tend birds for a few weeks in spring and autumn, earning 6d. or 8d. a day, or leading horses during harvest; only from the age of 13 were they ready for heavier work. Women and girls were employed only at harvest time. Given existing custom and practice, Rowley thought it undesirable to place any statutory restriction on the hours of work of either children or women. Labourers living in their own cottages could earn 14s. to 16s. a

*Figure 73* A prosperous farming family posing at Inkersall Farm, Staveley, where the Cavendishes owned the former Frescheville estate.

week; single men living in could make between £8 and £16 a year, plus board and lodging; they were engaged at statute fairs still at that period being held in neighbouring towns. It was a world which in the 1860s was about to be transformed, although not entirely swept away, by the growth of large-scale coal mining.[77]

The census figures of the mid-19th century add precision to comments such as Rowley's. Of the two dozen households making up the small village of Stainsby in 1871, seven were headed by farmers, five by farm labourers and three by men employed on the Hardwick estate. The only tradesmen were two shoemakers and a stonemason. Half the heads of household had been born in Ault Hucknall parish and all but four of the others nearby in either Derbyshire or Nottinghamshire. In 1901, when there were 21 households in the village, nine were headed by farmers. There were also three miners, a colliery labourer, a colliery blacksmith and a railway labourer, but the character of the place had hardly been transformed by the arrival of large-scale coalmining nearby. Two-thirds of the heads of household had been born in or near Ault Hucknall.[78]

Heath was a more mixed community, even before Holmewood colliery opened. In 1851, of the 75 households in the parish 19 were headed by men who described themselves as a 'farmer', a term that covered holdings ranging in size from four to 150 acres. Another 20 heads of household were agricultural labourers. Occupations among the other half of the community included six coalminers and smaller numbers of framework knitters, shoemakers, blacksmiths and other tradesmen. The picture was much the same a generation later, in 1881, although by then there were rather more coalminers. Only in the 1901 census, when 44 of the 119 heads of household were miners, 32 had other jobs at local collieries, and seven worked on the railway, were there signs that the community was changing.[79]

### Hardwick Hall and the Park

In the early 19th century routine expenditure at Hardwick on wages, food and drink, repairs and similar items, together with the cost of maintaining the park, was about £1,000 a year. This figure increased sharply when the 6th duke was in residence at the Hall. In 1819-21 household payments averaged £2,425, compared with £830 for years either side. Expenditure was also much higher in 1857-8, when the 6th duke was at Hardwick for the last couple of years of his life and payments averaged £3,700, compared with £900 a year over the previous five years. The only other years in which expenditure rose much above £1,000 were 1835 and 1843-7 (in each case to about £1,400 a year), when presumably the duke was also resident for longer than usual.[80]

The running costs at Hardwick fell after 1858 but rose again from 1868, when the estate was handed to the marquess of Hartington. Expenditure on game increased almost fourfold, to an average of £1,080 a year between 1868 and 1878, compared with £265 in the 10 years up to 1867. Hartington also established hunting stables at Hardwick, on which he spent an average of £730 a year between 1868 and 1876. The Hardwick collection disbursements include a subscription (initially £70, later £100) to the Rufford Hunt annually from 1859 until the end of the surviving accounts in 1878. During Lord Hartington's period it would be fair to describe Hardwick as a typical 19th-century sporting estate, which appears not to have been the case in the 6th and 7th dukes' time. Net expenditure on the stables at Hardwick was £2,370 in 1892, the first year after Hartington succeeded to the dukedom, but thereafter fell steadily to £660 in 1912 and only £220 in 1917. Other outdoor expenses remained largely unchanged during the same period.

Household expenditure during Lord Hartington's time was somewhat higher than before 1868 (an average of £1,390 a year, compared with £1,025 over the 10 years in which the estate was in his father's hands). This suggests slightly greater occupancy of the Hall by the family, but throughout the period covered by the annual accounts it seems clear that Hardwick remained mostly in the care of servants, with only occasional visits by either the 6th or 7th duke, or by Hartington. The small number of servants

*Figure 74*  The 8th
duke of Devonshire as
marquess of Hartington.
A leading Liberal Unionist
politician, Hartington was
given a life interest in the
Hardwick estate, which
he used as a country seat
until he succeeded his
father in 1891.

kept at Hardwick when none of the family was in residence is well
illustrated from census enumerations. In 1851 the Hall was in
the charge of a housekeeper (the widowed mother of the agent,
J.G. Cottingham), who had the help of three house-servants. All
the other servants needed when the house was occupied by the
duke would have travelled with him. In 1891, immediately before
Lord Hartington succeeded as 8th duke, the staff was slightly larger,
although when the family were in residence it would still have been
supplemented by a much greater number of travelling servants.
The housekeeper had six servants under her, including an usher of
the hall, and the outdoor staff included two gamekeepers, a head
gardener and a stud groom.[81]

In general, throughout the 19th and early 20th centuries, the
Hall, gardens and park ran at a loss and were subsidised by income
from rent and later royalties from coal mining. The income from
the estate was always well able to cover this loss, except in 1856-8,
when the 6th duke was in residence at Hardwick, and in 1858-60,
when the modernisation of the Hall was in progress. In those years
the Hardwick collection as a whole was in deficit and was being
subsidised by the rest of the family's estates.

Although the estate in hand generally ran at a loss, there was
some income to set against disbursements. The bulk of this came
from sales of timber and, in most years, a small surplus on the
home farm account, which included what was known technically
as 'agistment', the letting of grazing in the park to tenants. This
account consistently yielded about £400 a year net in the 1830s and
early 1840s. Between 1847 and 1868 the account was in surplus
in seven years and in deficit for the other 15, showing an average
net loss over the period as a whole of £100 a year. Under Lord
Hartington the position was reversed and except in 1873-4 the
account showed a profit of a couple of hundred pounds, as it did
between 1892 and 1917.

The explanation for the change in 1847 is that the estate gave up
farming at the Hall itself – the end of a tradition that went back to
the Middle Ages – and instead took one of the farms elsewhere in
Ault Hucknall in hand to manage as a home farm. In that year the
estate spent £551 on the buildings at Hucknall Farm (i.e. the farm
immediately to the east of Ault Hucknall church), and a further
£179 the following year. The amounts involved suggest that the
farm was almost completely reconstructed. Thereafter the net loss
on the Hucknall Farm account over the entire period between
1847 and 1878 averaged £220. In 1850-1 the buildings at Biggin
Farm, the estate's main holding in Tibshelf, were repaired at a cost
of £239 and in 1851-2 the farm appears to have been in hand,
since a 'Biggin Farm Account' showed a net loss of £511. This was

probably enough to bring the experiment to an end and thereafter only Hucknall Farm was run by the estate.

In the mid-1830s the estate opened and for a few years ran a colliery and brickyard at Holmewood. Neither was a success and in 1845 the colliery was let and the brickyard closed down. A new brickworks was built at Hardstoft in 1847-8, which remained in use until at least the late 1870s. Except in 1872-3, when it made a profit of £74, the yard was in deficit every year, the loss averaging £275 over the 31 years for which accounts are available. The works was clearly established to supply bricks, roof tiles and possibly also drain tiles to the estate, and may only have sold a small part of its output to outside customers.

Alongside the extensive programme of rebuilding on the let estate in the 1840s and 1850s, major work was also carried out at the Hall. The first indication of this appears in 1850-1, with payments of £195 on the kennels and buckroom and £115 on the park-keeper's house. About £110 was spent in 1852-3 on the greenhouse, water tank and elsewhere in the gardens, and on the great pond, bridge and road. In 1857-8 disbursements on repairs included £53 on Hardwick Lodge but the main outlay came the following year, when £3,732 was spent on new offices, windows, drains and other works at the Hall, £668 on the stables, kennel room etc., and £580 on new works to supply water to the Hall. In 1859-60 new building and repairs at the Hall, offices and stables cost a further £1,000; another £1,288 was spent on the waterworks, including £1,232 on a steam engine and boiler; and a duck decoy was built in the park at a cost of £591. The work appears to have been completed the following year, when £267 was spent on the Hall and £94 on the waterworks. Expenditure in later years seems to have been on normal repairs and renewals, rather than new work.

The 6th duke also made other improvements in the park besides the decoy. These included laying out new drives and avenues, planting square clumps of trees which became known as 'platoons' because of their shape, and building a sawmill and two new lodges (Norwood and Rowthorne) at the eastern entrances to the estate.[82]


## The Duke's Architects

The architect responsible for the modernisation of the Hall, and (latterly at least) for supervising work on the Hardwick estate during the 6th duke's time was Samuel Rollinson of Chesterfield, who was paid £73 in 1857-8, £203 the following year, and £93 over the two years 1860-2. Most of the individual payments making up these totals were for preparing plans, specifications and working drawings, and for supervising and inspecting finished work, relating to the rebuilding of farms and cottages in most of the villages on the Hardwick estate, and for some new building, although much of this work had been completed before 1857. In 1858-9, however, Rollinson was paid £50 for all the architectural work in connection with the rebuilding of the out-offices at the Hall, and also prepared drawings for a colonnade screen and a clock turret and alterations to the old barn there.[83]

*Figure 75* The sawmill close to Hardwick Hall, built as part of the 6th duke's estate improvements.

Rollinson appears to have been called in at a fairly late stage in the campaign of rebuilding on the estate, possibly mainly to inspect work that had already been completed to the design of the clerk of works. On the other hand, the discovery that he was also responsible for the extensive modernisation of a major 16th-century house rather lifts his reputation above the received view of him as a competent but not especially inspired designer of schools, moderniser of churches and supervisor of colliery housing schemes in north-east Derbyshire. The only other architects named in the accounts during the 6th duke's campaign of rebuilding on the Hardwick estate are Davies & Tew, also of Chesterfield, who in 1857-8 were paid £14 for a school at Hardstoft and some work on one of the farms at Stainsby. The 7th duke appears not to have continued with Rollinson's services but instead employed Charles Lindley of Mansfield to do more work on the service wing to the north of the hall.[84]

The heavy expenditure on both the farms and cottages and the mansion and park at Hardwick during the 6th duke's time partly mirrors what was being done elsewhere on the family's estates in this period, with extensive rebuilding at Chatsworth and elsewhere, and is an indication of the enormous wealth the duke had at his disposal. More generally, 'improvement' was in fashion on most great estates, or at least those that the resources to undertake such work, in the middle decades of the 19th century. On the other hand, the decision to spend money, on the scale it was spent, at Hardwick as well as Chatsworth, must also reflect the fondness the 6th duke felt for both houses.

The 6th duke succeeded to the title within two months of turning 21, before the estates could be resettled. This meant that he had greater freedom of action than most great landowners, although debt charges on the estate meant that he had only about forty per cent of the gross income to spend. For the rest of his life he showed considerable affection towards Hardwick, which he associated with his mother Georgiana. In 1832, for example, whilst entertaining the duchess of Kent and her daughter Princess Victoria at Chatsworth, he brought them over to Hardwick for the day. He himself spent short periods there for most of his life, although the house was too cold for longer stays. As we have seen, the duke undertook more extensive work on the house than any of his predecessors, and also had much of the Elizabethan needlework restored. He moved pictures and tapestries back and forth between Chatsworth and Hardwick, and brought some furniture over from Chatsworth, notably for the high great chamber at Hardwick. It is a sign of his interest in the place that his detailed *Handbook of Chatsworth and Hardwick* of 1844 includes both houses. During the Railway Mania of the 1840s the duke supported a scheme for a line from Ambergate to Buxton, even though it would have run through Chatsworth park, but opposed another abortive project for a railway from Chesterfield to Newark because it would have passed too close to Hardwick Hall. Finally, in 1858 the duke became the first head of his family since 1626 to die at Hardwick, rather than Chatsworth or one of their other houses.[85]

The 7th duke continued to make some improvements at Hardwick but appears to have lacked his predecessor's personal interest in the estate. This is illustrated not only in the falling off of expenditure after 1858 but also his decision to transfer Hardwick to his son as soon as he came of age in 1868. In turn, Lord Hartington's close connection with the estate, from which he drew an income of £4,000 a year, ended when he succeeded as 8th duke in 1891 and thereafter used Chatsworth as his principal country seat.

## THE GROWTH OF COAL MINING

Apart from the rebuilding and other improvements carried out in the mid-19th century, the other outstanding feature of this period in most of the parishes making up the Hardwick collection, mainly after 1870, was the growth of income from royalties, mineral rents and wayleaves as a result of the expansion of the coal industry. Although mining had co-existed with agriculture since the early 17th century, if not before, income from this source remained unimportant until well after 1800. The

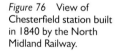

*Figure 76* View of Chesterfield station built in 1840 by the North Midland Railway.

only mining in the area in the early 19th century seems to have
been on the Oldcotes estate, at the northern end of Heath parish,
owned by the Pierrepont family of Thoresby in Sherwood Forest,
where there was a landsale pit, known as Oldcotes (although it
was some distance from the site of the mansion), operated by the
Greaves, Galloway and Goodwin families.[86]

This remained the position until the opening of the North
Midland Railway between Derby and Chesterfield in 1840, which led
to the sinking of small collieries to the east of the Rother, connected
by tramways to the main line. Major expansion of the coalfield
around Hardwick had to wait until a network of Midland Railway
branches was built to provide easier access to the market, and more
especially until much larger pits were sunk to the Top Hard coal
after 1870. Even then, the benefits derived by any one estate from the
growth of the industry might also depend on the success or failure
of a particular entrepreneur to whom they had leased their coal. In
this respect the Hardwick estate enjoyed slightly mixed fortunes until
larger companies entered the industry in the late 19th century.[87]

Between 1818 and 1850 royalties from coal mining yielded an
average of only £90 a year to the Hardwick collection, although
other income may have been returned within the figure for rent.
Between 1850 and 1870 the average was £240. This conceals a
fairly steady rise from about £130 a year to £480 over the 20 years,
whereas for the period up to 1850 the yearly figures fluctuate
sharply, with only a weak upward trend. By contrast, between 1870
and 1878 annual payments from coal royalties rose from £850 to
£3,200, or in other words from less than 10 per cent of the income
from rents to more than 30 per cent.

This increase was not simply a reflection of the cyclical boom in
mining in these years: it was the beginning of a process by which
income from coal would eventually overtake that from land. In 1892
royalties on the Hardwick estate totalled £7,107, or 55 per cent of
rents paid that year. Five years later the estate received nearly £11,000
from 'minerals' (almost all, presumably, from coal), compared with
just under £12,700 in rent. By 1902 rents had increased to £13,100
but royalties had reached almost £15,000. In 1907 the equivalent
figures were £13,400 and £18,400. In 1912 the gap had closed slightly,
with net income from minerals about £3,800 greater than rent, and
in 1917, under the artificial conditions of war-time, net royalties
were £15,750, compared with rents of £14,640.

When the surviving annual accounts open in 1818-19, the only
income recorded from coal came from a colliery in Blackwell, a
few miles to the south of Hardwick. In 1836-7, possibly because
of the news that the North Midland Railway was to be built close
by, the estate paid Thomas Sheppard and others £40 to try for

*Figure 77*   Hardwick colliery (always known locally as 'Holmewood'), showing the typical layout of a large, late 19th-century colliery with rail access from two companies' lines, empty and full sidings, and coke ovens and brickworks alongside the pit.

*Figure 78*   B Winning
colliery at Blackwell, one
of the first large modern
collieries to be opened on
the Hardwick estate.

coal at Holmewood, in the north-west corner of Ault Hucknall
parish. Both a colliery and brickyard were opened there but neither
prospered under direct management. In 1845 the colliery was let to
Joshua Thornally, who may have lacked sufficient working capital,
since he elected to pay £11 a year interest on the value of the
moveable plant and tools, rather than buy them outright. He made
small royalty payments (and kept up the interest payments) until
1860-1, when the colliery seems to have closed.

Mining was restarted at Holmewood by the Wingerworth Coal
Company, which paid a rent of £250 a year for coal in Heath and
Ault Hucknall between 1865 and 1873. During this period the
Wingerworth Company's main interests lay in the adjoining parish of
North Wingfield, exploiting coal beneath the estate belonging to the
Hunloke family of Wingerworth Hall. The business was divided in
1873, with a separation of a new colliery at Holmewood from the older
pits in North Wingfield. A new Hardwick Coal Company (controlled
by the same partners as the old company) paid a rent of £800 in
1873-4 and the following three years, which rose to £1,000 a year in
1877-8, the last year for which figures are available. A by-product
coking plant was added in 1912 to what was officially known as
Hardwick colliery, although locally it was always called Holmewood,
the name of the adjoining village built for miners there.[88]

The other large colliery enterprise on the Hardwick estate in this
period was at Blackwell, where Emerson Muschamp Bainbridge,
later to become better known as the founder of the Bolsover
Colliery Company, sank two collieries (A Winning and B Winning)
in the early 1870s. He began paying rent at £500 a year in 1870 and
by 1878 his payments had reached £1,500. On a smaller scale the
Pilsley Colliery Company, which opened a pit near the village of
that name in North Wingfield parish, was paying £300 a year from
1873-4 under a lease that also required them to supply coal free of
charge to Chatsworth, the value of which (between £23 and £107

a year in this period) was credited to the Hardwick estate account.
Why this condition should have been imposed on the Pilsley
company is unclear, unless it was simply that their pit was slightly
nearer Chatsworth than any of the others on the Hardwick estate.
Neither they nor any of the other companies seems to have been
required to supply coal to Hardwick.

## DOE LEA AND HOLMEWOOD

Of the colliery villages that grew up around Hardwick in the late
19th century to house miners who came to work at the new pits,
the two that lay closest to the park were Doe Lea, built just inside
Ault Hucknall parish on the east bank of the river from which it
was named, near the bridge carrying the Chesterfield-Mansfield
road over the river, and Holmewood, which took its name from
a nearby farm and straddled the boundary between Heath and
North Wingfield.

### Doe Lea

*Figure 79*   The grid-plan
street layout of the
Sheepbridge Company's
village at Doe Lea,
built for miners at
Glapwell colliery.

The origins of Doe Lea lay in the decision in 1872 of the Hallowes
family of Glapwell Hall to lease the coal beneath their estate to the
Sheepbridge Coal & Iron Company of Chesterfield. After some
delay in finding a suitable site for the pit that would not be visible

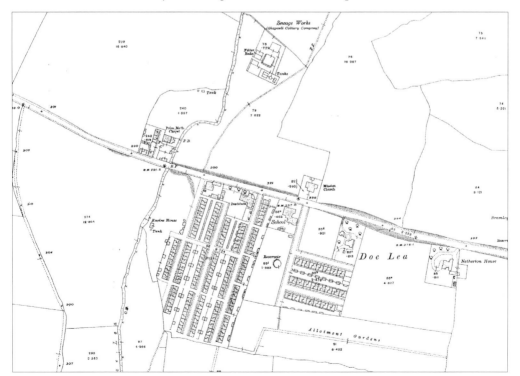

*Figure 80*   The gatepiers
which remain at the
entrance to Glapwell
Hall, demolished in the
early 1950s.

from the Hallowes' house, sinking began in 1882 on the north side
of the Mansfield road on the floor of the Doe Lea valley about a
mile west of Glapwell village. Three rows of sinkers' cottages were
built to the east of the later village of Doe the same year. Coal
began to be raised in 1884. The colliery was served by the Midland
Railway's single-track branch from Staveley to Bolsover, which was
extended to a new terminus alongside the Mansfield road, although
initially there was no passenger service on the line. More cottages
were built to house the miners, together with a school (in 1885)
and an Anglican mission room two years later.[89]

The main phase of building at Doe Lea dated from 1890, when
Sheepbridge agreed to erect a hundred cottages at a cost of £15,000,
most of which were occupied by the time the census was taken
early the following year. In the meantime the railway was extended
to Pleasley and a passenger service established. Initially the nearest
station was at Rowthorne rather than at the colliery, where a
station was only opened in 1892. The layout of the village followed
the pattern adopted elsewhere by both Sheepbridge and other
companies in the Derbyshire coalfield, with blocks of terraced
cottages arranged in long, straight rows set at right-angles to the
main road, from which access was provided by East Street and West
Street at either end of the village.

When Doe Lea was enumerated for the 1891 census, it was
found that about half the inhabitants had been born locally and
the other half from further afield, although only 13 had come
from more than 50 miles away, including one man born in
Ireland and another from Berkshire. Six families gave Willenhall,
in the South Staffordshire coalfield, as their birthplace, which
suggests that Sheepbridge had been deliberately recruiting
miners for the new pit in one of the declining coalfields of the
Black Country. Quite a few families had moved from elsewhere
on the western side of the Derbyshire coalfield, where pits sunk
to shallow seams in the early 19th century were closing. This
pattern of relatively short-distance migration from within the
same district to new pits offering the prospect of better working
conditions, better earnings and possibly better housing was
also evident at Bolsover in the same period and may well be
characteristic of all the villages on the concealed coalfield of the
magnesian limestone.[90]

As in other colliery housing schemes in the area, of which only
those of the Bolsover Company at New Bolsover and Creswell
could be described as 'model villages', living conditions in fact
remained poor. In the summer of 1893 seven cases of typhoid and
11 of scarlet fever were reported in Doe Lea, both of which the
local medical officer of health attributed to the poor construction

# Sporting Life

Figure A   *Holmewood Cricket Team photographed in the 1920s.*

Figure B   *Hardwick Colliery Football Team, posing outside the* Holmewood Hotel *in Devonshire Terrace, Holmewood, in 1917.*

There was a strong sporting tradition in north Derbyshire pit villages. The communities on the Hardwick estate were no exception. Cricket was especially prominent and there was a long standing view in the game that coal miners made good fast bowlers, due to the rigours of the coal face which demanded a sturdy physique and endless stamina. These essential qualities were clearly exemplified by well-known Derbyshire-born professionals such as Les Jackson and Cliff Gladwin. The colliery companies generally encouraged the setting up of cricket clubs, presumably seeing the fresh air and exercise away from the gloom of the pit as a positive contribution to a happy workforce. Glapwell colliery ran two teams, a senior one in the more highly-graded Derbyshire League and a second XI in the local Scarcliffe and District League. The colliery manager was invariably among the club officials in the early 1900s.

Unfortunately, records of sporting organisations rarely survive in any quantity. Small village clubs generally lacked their own premises and as committee members came and went, so minutes, financial records, evidence of fixtures and results, and publicity material were often lost. To a degree this situation was magnified in the mining areas where sporting organisations reflected the overall rise and fall of the coal industry, with many clubs disappearing along with the pits. In these circumstances, local weekly newspapers supply some of the information no longer available from club records. Anyone

interested in researching any aspect of local sport would do well to turn to the sports pages – not always at the back in the early 1900s.

Because Hardwick was so close to the Nottinghamshire boundary, the Mansfield and Chesterfield papers vied for the local readership, and so fixtures in Glapwell and Doe Lea were covered by the *Mansfield Chronicle* and *Mansfield Reporter* as well as the *Derbyshire Times*. In the 1890s and the 1900s the two colliery cricket teams were permanent features of the sporting scene and their fixtures were faithfully covered. The cricket club had a regular annual dinner and periodic fund-raising events at the *Young Vanish* pub in Glapwell – named after a racehorse owned by the Hallowes family of Glapwell Hall – and these also were usually reported.

In this period, football was less prominent. A club would start out on a wave of enthusiasm, but one poor season or the loss of a key organiser, and it would fade from the scene. Doe Lea Primitive Methodist Chapel ran a team for a short time, beginning by playing the occasional friendly match, but by 1900 was playing in the local Scarcliffe League where opponents included Sutton Parish Church and Bolsover Colliery Reserves. Rather oddly, the colliery did not sponsor an official team then, but more recently the village has been notable in managing to sustain a team that competes on an equal basis with clubs from much larger places in the 'pyramid' of competitions that can eventually lead to Football League status.

of the earth closets. Sheepbridge agreed later the same year to improve sewerage and sewage disposal in the village.

The completion of the housing led to better provision for education and worship. In 1892 the duke of Devonshire, Brabazon Hallowes of Glapwell Hall and the Sheepbridge Company agreed to share the cost of a new school for 250 children, and in the same year a Primitive Methodist chapel was built. In 1895 the vicar of Ault Hucknall asked the Sheepbridge Company for a site for a new mission room, to replace the temporary building of 1887. Life in the 1890s, beyond the confines of the pit, very much revolved around the two churches, the venue for regular concerts, dances and later lantern slide shows. By 1895 the colliery was running a cricket team, which played initially in the Scarcliffe league, and for a short time there was also a Doe Lea Primitive Methodist football team. This was superseded by a longer-lived Glapwell colliery team, which played first in the Lampson junior league but later in the Chesterfield minor league, where they met local rivals Hardwick colliery. Opportunities for recreation outside the village were limited before the coming of a Chesterfield-Mansfield bus service after the First World War, with only three trains a day on the railway through Glapwell. In 1897 excursion trains to Manchester and to the pantomime at Sheffield were advertised.

A major development came in 1904 with the opening of the Glapwell colliery institute, built at a cost of £2,500 by the Sheepbridge Company. This provided a much bigger social centre for the village, with a billiard room and a library as well as a licensed bar. By this period social life had developed considerably, with the establishment of a brass band and ambulance classes at the colliery, an Oddfellows lodge that met at the *Young Vanish* pub in Glapwell, and evening continuation classes at the schools, as well as the longer-established football and cricket teams.

## Holmewood

The village of Holmewood was built to house miners at Holmewood colliery itself and also at the Hardwick Coal Company's other pit nearby at Williamthorpe, sunk in 1901-4 on the Hunloke family's estate. It was laid out on previously unoccupied land to the north of Heath Road, on the edge of Heath parish, immediately to the east of some older cottages (Hunloke Road, which lay just inside North Wingfield) built by the Wingerworth Company. At the time sinking began at Williamthorpe, the Wingerworth and Hardwick companies were reconstructed again and the business incorporated as the Hardwick Colliery Company Ltd. At the same time its operations

*Figure 81* Holmewood, built by the Wingerworth Coal Company to house miners employed at the nearby colliery, showing the rectilinear grid plan used by almost all companies in the Derbyshire coalfield.

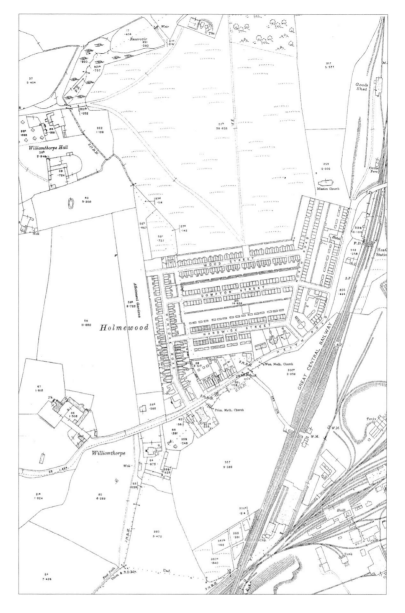

were reorganised. The smaller, older pits to the west were either closed or disposed of, and resources concentrated on developing Holmewood and Williamthorpe.[91]

Holmewood initially consisted of three parallel roads running from west to east (Hardwick Street, Compton Street and Wood Street), flanked by Hunloke Road to the west and North Road to the east. Other houses were built along Heath Road itself. The houses were of brick, arranged in terraces with privies and coalhouses across a yard to the rear. Those on Compton Street

*Figure 82* Devonshire Terrace, some of the better-class housing fronting the main road through Holmewood.

and North Street were four-roomed, whereas those on Wood Street had a small kitchen to the rear. The older houses on Hunloke Road had slightly larger kitchens, and some better-class housing for officials was built on Hardwick Street and Devonshire Terrace (i.e. Heath Road).[92]

As well as the houses and shops, two Methodist churches were built on Heath Road and an Anglican mission church, St Alban's, erected to the north of North Street in 1896. In 1905 a large block of schools was opened at the junction of Heath Road and Slack Lane, about halfway between Holmewood and the older village of Heath, where there was no new building in this period connected with the colliery. Like Doe Lea, Holmewood was built by a colliery company with only a limited link to the Devonshire estate, through its ownership of Holmewood colliery. The royalties from Williamthorpe colliery went to the Hunlokes of Wingerworth Hall, just as some of those from Glapwell went to the Hallowes family. On the other hand, the building of Holmewood substantially changed the character of the parish in which most of the houses lay, as well as greatly increasing its population.

## SCHOOLS, CHURCHES, CHAPELS AND CHARITY

Alongside the increase in expenditure on the rebuilding of farms on the estate, the other marked change in the Hardwick collection during the 19th century is the growth of expenditure on schools, churches and general charitable giving. The amounts involved were much smaller than those spent on the farms and at the Hall, but the pattern is one of steady growth, instead of the sharp increase in repairs and rebuilding during the later years of the 6th duke, followed by stability under the 7th duke and Lord Hartington. Some of the expenditure, towards the end of the 19th century, was connected with the expansion of coal mining and the building of new villages to house the miners. Most, however, was simply the family's contribution to a slow process of modernisation on what remained predominantly a rural estate. Outside the mining villages there was little population growth and so only modest new work was required. Where large sums had to be spent quickly, as at Doe Lea and Holmewood, others were also involved, mainly the colliery companies and (in the case of education after 1903) the county council.[93]

In the early 19th century the estate's only contribution towards education in the parishes around Hardwick was a gratuity of £10 a year to the school near the Hall established in 1724 and interest on the legacy left by John Phillips in 1734. In the 1830s the school continued to be supported partly from endowments and partly by payments by parents. The endowment income was about £25 a year in the 1850s and from 1850-1 the estate was contributing to the master's salary at Hardwick beyond the traditional gift of £10 a year.[94]

In 1825 the 6th duke built a school at Upper Langwith, to which he gave £15 a year. In 1833 the estate made a donation of £10 made towards the building of a Sunday school at Hardstoft, and from 1835-6 gave two guineas towards teaching 15 poor children in Tibshelf. A regular payment of £15 a year also began to a schoolmaster at Blackwell.[95]

At Heath there were two or three dame schools for infants in the early 19th century and one school for older children, which in 1833 had 20 pupils, 17 of them boys. When this school was established is not clear but in 1821 it moved into new premises near the parsonage. From 1838 the estate paid for repairs at the school, and from 1849 made up the master's salary and refunded the rent for the schoolroom. During this period Heath school was said to have an endowment of £15 a year from the Devonshire charity established in 1687, although it was the poor of the parish, rather than a school, who were mentioned in the

*Figure 83* St Alban's, the Anglican mission church built to serve Holmewood.

*Figure 84*  The schoolmaster's house and part of the school house at Heath.

wills of the two benefactors. In the 1840s the vicar was giving an additional £5 a year, which enabled 20 poor children to be taught free. The schoolroom was improved and enlarged in 1867 at a cost of £366.[96]

All the schools on the estate benefited from the improvements carried through on the estate in the 1850s. In 1858 a new school was built at Hardstoft, presumably replacing the old Sunday school there. This was the gift of Lady Louisa Cavendish, who in 1862 was described as its principal supporter. In the latter year the 7th duke erected a new school, with a house for the master, near the site of the medieval manor house at Stainsby. This replaced the building on the edge of the park, which became a private residence. A nominal rent of £5 a year for Hardstoft school was reimbursed from 1860 and another for Stainsby from the following year. In 1870 the Hardstoft school was being used for the girls of the parish of Ault Hucknall and Stainsby for the boys.[97]

By 1864 regular support to schools in the Hardwick collection had reached £119. Apart from the building work at Heath in 1867, and a donation of £150 towards a new school at Scarcliffe the following year, there were no further one-off payments during the

*Figure 85* The small wayside schoolroom at Hardstoft, also used for Anglican services.

7th duke's time, although an annual donation of £10 to Scarcliffe National school was instituted in 1869.

After the passing of the Elementary Education Act in 1870, Stainsby school began to receive an Education Department grant, which was retained by the estate, presumably because it was guaranteeing the master's salary. 'Repairs' at the school costing £58 in 1872 may in fact have been improvements required by the department to secure recognition. In the early 1870s small donations were made to several schools in the area, probably also to help fund improvements required by the Act. In 1877, the last year for which detailed figures are available, the Hardwick collection gave £56 10s. towards the running costs of Hardwick school, £26 and £14 to make up the salaries at Hardstoft and Heath respectively, £5 each in remitted rents at Heath, Hardstoft and Stainsby and £3 at Langwith, and £44 in subscriptions to Blackwell, Tibshelf, Shirebrook and Scarcliffe day schools and Ault Hucknall Sunday school, a total commitment of £159.

By this period more radical changes were about to occur as a result of the building of the village at Doe Lea. When the needs of Ault Hucknall parish were surveyed under the 1870 Act it was found that nearly all the children living there were of the class who would attend an elementary school and that 110 places were required. These could be supplied by the existing boys' school at Stainsby and the girls' and infant school at Hardstoft. Both were described as Church of England, rather than National, schools. When sinking began at Glapwell colliery in 1882 the ratepayers of Ault Hucknall and Glapwell objected to the two townships being made into a single school district, presumably fearing that a school board would be created and a rate levied to build and maintain a new school. The vicar of Ault Hucknall, Henry Cottingham, agreed that further accommodation would be needed once the pit opened, although he suggested that children from Rowthorne could attend a new school proposed for Pleasley. In 1875 Cottingham reported that the schools planned for Ault Hucknall had not yet been built but would be as soon as the colliery opened. Once it had opened, the owners, the Sheepbridge Company, gave £20 towards the cost of a temporary school at Doe Lea and £25 a year towards the salary of a mistress. The Hardwick estate also contributed.[98]

*Figure 86* The infant school at Rowthorne, built to ease overcrowding at other local schools as the population of the area rose.

In 1884 Brabazon Hallowes, the sole landowner in Glapwell and also the owner of the coal being mined by Sheepbridge, agreed to build a permanent school for 100 children at Doe Lea, where the 32 miners' cottages erected by that date had a population of 250. His offer was conditional on assistance being

forthcoming from the company and also on the understanding
that Lord Hartington went ahead with his plan to build a school
at Rowthorne. Hallowes calculated that there were 230 children
of school age in Ault Hucknall and Glapwell, of whom only 11
lived at Glapwell itself. Of the rest, 29 lived at Rowthorne, 91
at Hardstoft, 32 at Stainsby and 66 at Doe Lea. The Education
Department, where the question was settled at ministerial level,
presumably because of Hartington's involvement, agreed to
this scheme and an infant school for 50 children was opened at
Rowthorne in 1885.

With the continued growth of Doe Lea these arrangements
soon proved inadequate. In July 1892 Cottingham submitted
plans for an extension to the school there to bring the total
accommodation to 250 children above infant age. By the
following January this project, dependent on support from
Hallowes (who in the meantime had died), the duke of
Devonshire (as Hartington had become two years before)
and Sheepbridge, had collapsed because of the company's
withdrawal, leaving no option but to establish a school board.
The duke also refused to increase his support for the voluntary
schools at Heath and Ault Hucknall. Since there was no school
at all in Glapwell and no boys' school at Heath, the most
convenient arrangement was to make Ault Hucknall, Glapwell
and Heath a united district. Meetings in the first two parishes

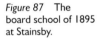

*Figure 87* The
board school of 1895
at Stainsby.

*Figure 88* The imposing block of county council schools at Holmewood (although named Heath Schools) built to serve the new village there in 1904. This remained a large, all-age school until after

voted in favour of this plan; Heath, which received no rate income from Glapwell colliery and whose boys attended the school at Stainsby, were opposed and proceeded to close their own school. The department therefore issued notices for the compulsory establishment of a board. Once again the vice-president, C.T. Ritchie, was consulted, no doubt because one of his ministerial colleagues was personally concerned.

In 1893 the new board for Ault Hucknall, Glapwell and Heath took over the duke of Devonshire's schools at Heath, Stainsby and Rowthorne and the school at Doe Lea belonging to the Hallowes estate. At the time of the transfer all four were Church of England schools. The Church school at Hardstoft continued on a voluntary basis. Two years later the board pulled down the school at Stainsby and replaced it with a larger building. The Church of England school at Hardstoft, which was also used for services on Sunday evenings, was rebuilt in 1894, and the school at Doe Lea four years later.[99]

After 1903, when county councils took over former board schools and more generous funding for Church schools was introduced, the estate's subscriptions fell away at once. Whereas in 1902 the Hardwick collection gave £112 to schools, in 1907 the figure was £8 and remained at that level until after the First World War. When new schools were needed at Heath, following the building of the village of Holmewood, or at Upper Langwith, with the growth of the railway village at Langwith Junction, both around 1900, it was the county council that undertook the work, unaided (except through the rates) by the principal local landowner.

## Support for Local Churches

After the flurry of work stimulated by Archdeacon Butler's visitation of 1823, the estate did nothing further to support local churches until 1839, when it paid for repairs to the vestry at Heath. In 1848 it gave £5 towards the cost of restoring the bells at Tibshelf, and both then and in the following year gave the same amount towards an organ for Ault Hucknall. Also in 1849, £11 was spent on a stove for the chancel at Ault Hucknall. In 1851 the estate paid H.I. Stevens's fee (£17) as architect for the restoration of Ault Hucknall and a year later gave a further £5 towards the organ fund there, as well as £10 towards a stained glass window at Heath.

By far the largest item of expenditure came in 1854, when the 6th duke subscribed £700 towards the cost of a completely new church (also by Stevens) at Heath, gave materials worth £15, and spent £68 on the churchyard wall. The new church was built at the northern end of the main village street, in very much the position a medieval church might have stood, had Heath ever had a church of its own. The old church, the last remaining building on the site of the deserted village of Lound, was taken down and some of the masonry used to build a small mortuary chapel to serve the burial ground there, which remained open.

*Figure 89* Heath Vicarage, later demolished and replaced with a close of private houses.

*Figure 90* Langwith Rectory, a handsome building very similar in style to the Vicarage at Heath. It accommodated the minister of a small but wealthy living.

The estate continued to make small contributions to local churches and parsonages during Lord Hartington's time, but the only major expenditure was on a new parsonage at Langwith, costing £1,564, in 1867, and another at Heath. The two are similar in style and are probably by the same architect. Both have been replaced in recent times by new parsonages and the house at Heath demolished. The Old Rectory at Langwith remains a private residence.[100]

Until the building of Doe Lea and Holmewood, both of which acquired Anglican mission churches as soon as the population began to arrive, there was little call for church extension in either Heath or Ault Hucknall. The school built at Hardstoft in 1858 was licensed for worship and from 1868 the estate gave £5 a year for several years to the master of Hardstoft school for his work with the choir there. It was still being used as a mission room in 1912.[101]

The only donation to a nonconformist place of worship recorded in the estate accounts for this period was a gift of £150 to the Wesleyan chapel at Blackwell in 1874-5. This contrasts with the regular, if generally small, payments to parish churches in the area but probably reflects the lack of support for nonconformity in the purely agricultural villages in the collection, rather than any hostility on the part of the dukes towards Dissent. Until the building of Doe Lea and Holmewood, where in both cases Methodist chapels were established early on, the only

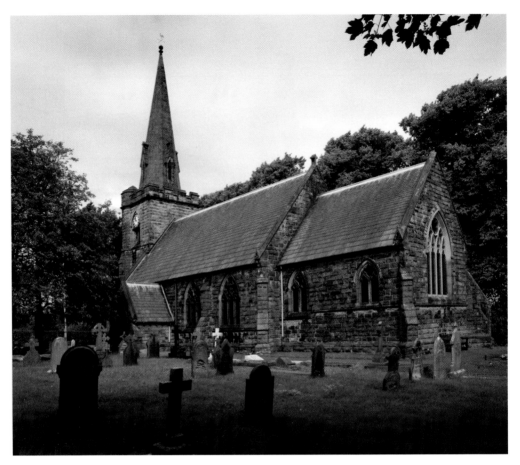

*Figure 91*  All Saints',
Heath, built in 1852 to
replace the old church
a short distance away,
which was demolished.

nonconformist place of worship in the area was a Methodist New
Connexion chapel at Hardstoft, built in 1835. This had about
50 sittings and standing room for 60; on Census Sunday in 1851
it had an afternoon congregation of 40 and a Sunday school of
similar size in the morning, afternoon and evening. The chapel
was still in use around 1860 but seems to have no later history.[102]

After 1892 the estate gave few hundred pounds a year up to the
First World War to what were described in the summary accounts
merely as 'churches and chapels'.

The two parishes at the heart of the Hardwick estate, Ault
Hucknall and Heath, continued to benefit in the 19th century from
the charity established in 1687. Neither had much else in the way
of endowed charities, apart from small shares in Francis Gisborne's
charity which served a large number of Derbyshire parishes and,
in the case of Ault Hucknall, a fund established by William Derrey
in 1794, which produced an income of £3 3s. 4d. a year, distributed
to the poor at Easter in doles of a few shillings each. In the early
19th century, £18 a year from the earl and countess of Devonshire's

charity was appropriated to Heath and Langwith and a similar sum divided between the villages in Ault Hucknall and the hamlet of Stony Houghton. The money was used to bind apprentices at premiums of £5 or £6 each. In 1826 sums of £123 and £45 respectively were taken from the charity's accumulated funds to pay for the new schoolroom at Langwith and repairs to the schoolhouse in Hardwick park. This the Charity Commissioners considered disproportionate to the income available, although in later years payments continued to be made to local schools from what was now known as the Hardwick Apprenticing Charity.[103]

## Individual Gifts

Other gifts would have been made privately by the dukes or other members of the family and thus do not appear in the collection accounts. As in previous centuries, there were casual payments to individuals and families who had suffered loss, as well as regular 'gratuities' to old servants, which gradually evolved into pensions charged on the collection account.

Philanthropic payments included a regular subscription of £5 a year to clothing clubs in Ault Hucknall and Heath, starting in 1850. In the same year the estate made a loan of £20 to Christopher Hall to enable him to emigrate. There is no sign of more organised emigration from the district under the 6th duke's auspices, although the parish overseers could also pay for emigration. Other one-off expenses included £30 for coronation celebrations in all the townships in the collection in 1838, and gifts totalling £25 to support rejoicing at the marriage of the Prince of Wales in Blackwell, Heath and Ault Hucknall in 1862, plus a further £17 for fireworks in the two latter parishes. In 1870 the 7th duke gave what seems the fairly modest sum of £25 to the Renishaw Colliery Explosion Fund, although the estate had little direct interest in that district. Two years later he subscribed £100 towards the Chesterfield Hospital building fund and in 1875 gave £50 to a similar fund at Mansfield Woodhouse. The duke also gave an annual subscription of £5 to Chesterfield Hospital.

'Other subscriptions and donations' absorbed a few hundred pounds in the Hardwick collection each year between 1892 and 1912, but rose to £865 in 1917, because of appeals connected with the war.

## A Local Balance Sheet

As with the earlier estate accounts, it is possible to analyse the 19th-century material to compare the amount collected by the

estate in rent, coal royalties and other income with the amount
ploughed back into the local community through wages, the
purchase of goods and services, and charitable giving. Spending
on the Hardwick estate certainly increased in the mid-19th
century, both in support for schools and churches and in the
improvement of the fixed capital of the estate, but this should be
set against an increase in income, not matched by any growth in
acreage, and much of it derived from coal royalties rather than
rent. Similarly, before dismissing Lord Hartington's development
of the estate for hunting and shooting after 1869 as an example of
the idle rich enjoying themselves at the expense of the labouring
poor, it is worth remembering that much of the expenditure
involved would have found its way back into the local economy.

A reasonably accurate measure of income and expenditure in
the Hardwick collection between 1818 and 1878 can be obtained
by comparing receipts with payments recorded in the annual
accounts. This approach is not beyond criticism but it produces
a clearer picture than a purely impressionistic discussion. Some
inaccuracy is inevitable: part of the profit on the wood account,
for example, was earned outside the Hardwick collection
(although still in north-east Derbyshire); more seriously, some
of the disbursements were paid to creditors outside the district.
The most obvious example of this is county and national
taxation. In any case it is impracticable to define a 'local
economy' in terms of parish boundaries and to seek to measure
the estate's spending within that area. All one can sensibly do
is estimate roughly what proportion of the estate's income was
spent in the district from which it was drawn. The results of
such an exercise are reasonably clear-cut and show how the
Hardwick estate in the 19th century developed from what may
well have been its lowest ebb, in terms of impact on the local
community, in the second half of the 18th century. The 60 years
for which detailed information is available divide fairly clearly
into three phases.

Until the 6th duke's campaign of rebuilding, combined with
draining and other improvements, got fully underway around
1848, payments represented on average 35 per cent of receipts
each year. The figure rose to just over 50 per cent in years in
which the duke spent some time at Hardwick, and fell below
30 per cent in a few years, for example immediately following a
rent increase in 1829-30, when payments did not rise in line with
a one-off growth in income. In general, a larger proportion of
receipts (which were themselves much increased on the figure for
the mid-18th century) were being spent locally between 1818 and
1847 than before 1800, and a smaller proportion remitted from

the estate to the duke to spend either at Chatsworth or in London or elsewhere.

The increase, as we have seen, was distributed over a range of expenditure, some on the Hall and the demesne estate, some on the farms, and a little on the community as a whole. Most would be described in modern terms as spending on current consumption (especially the additional payments on the household in years in which the duke was in residence), rather than on capital improvements that would themselves later generate additional income, but most would have returned money to the local economy through wages and the purchase of goods and services.

Between 1848 and 1861 payments at Hardwick averaged no less than 93 per cent of receipts; in the last five of those years they exceeded receipts, with expenditure averaging 129 per cent of income. This was the period of the 6th duke's great rebuilding of the Hardwick estate, which eventually, just before his death, embraced the Hall as well as the farms and cottages. Besides new building, these years also saw a lengthy campaign of under-draining and other improvements, the cost of which greatly overshadowed the steady increase in spending on schools and churches.

During these years almost all the income from the Hardwick collection was being ploughed back into it, and for part of the time money was being transferred to Hardwick from elsewhere. Much of this expenditure went on improvements to the land and buildings of permanent value. Indeed, this was the argument normally advanced by landowners or their agents in favour of spending large sums on draining and rebuilding in this period: better farms attracted better tenants who paid better rents. The success of the 6th duke's policy can be seen in the imposition of a major rent increase in 1855-6, which was carried through with only a slight rise in arrears. This in turn suggests that few tenants left because of the increase in rent. In other words, the duke had the resources to carry out the improvements and his tenants had the means to pay him back through higher rents. If their ability to pay higher rents is an indication of rising returns to farmers, then part of these increased profits would have found their way back into the local economy, through spending by the farmers themselves and through wages paid to their labourers.

It is possible to argue that the Hardwick collection itself had the resources to fund the improvements, since up to 1856 total expenditure remained below total income, and only rose above it between 1857 and 1861 because of the work carried out at the Hall. This was only the case because the owner of the estate had ample resources from elsewhere to maintain his income and could afford to draw a much reduced figure from Hardwick for a decade or so. The same argument applies with greater force to the modernisation of the Hall, which put the collection into deficit for the only time in its history. If Hardwick had been an estate in its own right, its owner would only have been able to rebuild the mansion on the scale undertaken by the 6th duke by borrowing, presumably in the form of a mortgage charged on future rent income. As it was, transfers from elsewhere ensured that the rebuilding could be carried out without encumbering the estate in that way.

## An Unproductive Investment

What can be claimed with more justification is that the expenditure on Hardwick Hall was an unproductive investment, compared with the money spent on the farms. The 6th duke never intended to make Hardwick his main home, nor does it appear that he planned to let the mansion and grounds, even to a member of his own family. The modernisation was simply to make the house more comfortable for occasional visits by the duke and his family, and, it might be added, for the servants who lived there all the time, since the improvements consisted chiefly of new offices.

Once the modernisation of the Hall had been paid for, the 7th duke reduced expenditure of all kinds on the Hardwick collection and between 1862 and 1868 payments represented an average of 65 per cent of receipts, half the figure of the years up to 1861. Expenditure increased after Lord Hartington took over the estate in 1868, but, certainly until the surviving accounts end in 1878, remained at an average of 65 per cent of receipts. The explanation for this, of course, is that receipts also increased during Hartington's time, chiefly from coal royalties, and that this enabled him to spend much larger sums than his father had on the household, game and stables.

Viewed in this light, Hardwick in the 1870s and 1880s can be represented as a landed estate whose occupier indulged in conspicuous consumption at the expense not so much of his father's tenant farmers or their labourers, as the lessees of his coal and their miners. Much of this spending would have been returned to the local economy through increased employment at Hardwick when Hartington was in residence, whereas earlier generations of the family had drawn income from the estate and spent it in London. Spending on repairs and other improvements to the estate also continued in the 1870s, if on a much smaller scale than in the 6th duke's day, but with no further large-scale, 'unproductive' expenditure on the Hall. Overall, the local community probably benefited from having a member of the family resident even for short periods at Hardwick, especially one who gave large hunting and shooting parties, compared with the pattern in the 18th and early 19th centuries, when the family visited only occasionally. Although the percentage of receipts disbursed locally from 1862 was only two thirds of the figure for the period between 1847 and 1861, it was between two and three times the proportion spent 50 or 100 years earlier.

# Chapter 7

# Hardwick in the Twentieth Century

*Figure 92* Hardwick Hall from the south, framed by the hornbeam hedges planted by the 6th Duke's niece, Lady Louisa Cavendish, who occupied the hall in the late 19th century.

Like that of almost all communities in England, the history of the villages around Hardwick in the 20th century falls into two contrasting halves, divided by the Second World War. Hardwick itself, which survived the First World War more or less unscathed, could not escape the impact of that of 1939-45 (and the Labour government which came afterwards). As elsewhere in the Derbyshire coalfield, the area around the Hall passed through substantial change after 1945. From the end of the war until about 1970, the district was dominated by the coal industry but, towards the end of the 20th century, former mining communities fell into decay as central and local government sought to solve seemingly intractable economic and social problems arising from the decline of coal. Conversely, villages untouched by the industry prospered in those years.

## HALL, PARK AND ESTATE

After the 8th duke succeeded to the title in 1891 Hardwick reverted to being used by the family for only a few weeks of the year, or was occupied by junior branches of the family. Thus for several years up to her death in 1907 the 8th duke lent Hardwick each summer to his sister Louisa and her husband Admiral Francis Egerton. Lady Louisa's most important contribution to Hardwick dates from some years before, with the creation of the present main garden to the south of the house in about 1870. This occupies the site of the original garden but its plan, with cross-shaped walks between yew and hornbeam hedges, was entirely due to her.[104]

The 8th duke died in 1908 and was succeeded by a nephew, Victor Cavendish, the eldest son of Lord Edward Cavendish, the 7th duke's third son. The 9th duke spent a few weeks every autumn at Hardwick for a shooting party and in some years the family, including seven children, were at Hardwick for Christmas. On those occasions the house was fully occupied by family, guests and servants. At other times the house was left in the care of an 'odd man', two housemaids and a daily cleaner; all the other servants travelled with the family to whichever house they were occupying at a particular time. Before the First World War, in addition to the female staff, the family generally brought a few male servants with them to Hardwick: the butler, the groom of the chambers, the duke's valet and two footmen.

149

Duchess Evelyn, the 9th duke's wife, took a keen interest in the furnishings at Hardwick, especially the tapestry, on which she did a great deal of careful restoration work. During her short marriage to Lord Curzon (1917-25) his second wife, an American who preferred Hackwood to Kedleston, drove over to Hardwick for the day while they were staying at Chatsworth. She admitted that the duchess had made Hardwick 'most beautiful' and thought it 'the most lovely and romantic house I have ever seen'. She did observe, however, that although it had originally been built 'in the midst of unspoilt green country', it was now entirely surrounded by coal mines: 'Even the trees are black and the Duchess complained of the difficulty of having everything kept clean'. When the 9th duke died in 1938 he left Hardwick to his widow as a dower house and Duchess Evelyn remained there, except during the Second World War, until the mansion and park passed to the National Trust in 1959. She stayed on as the trust's tenant until her own death in 1960, although in later years she visited the house comparatively little.[105]

*Figure 93* Evelyn, duchess of Devonshire, the widow of the 9th duke who made Hardwick her home for many years, shown repairing tapestries at the Hall. The results of this task, to which she devoted much time and effort, can be seen today.

*Figure 94*  The impressive Wine-Glass avenue of limes, originally planted in the 1920s by Duchess Evelyn on open land east of the house, probably to hide the surrounding colliery landscape, and later restored after war-time damage.

Until Hardwick came into the hands of the National Trust the house had never been shown to the public, although the grounds were opened. The mansion was not pressed into service during the First World War but during the Second World War much of the park was requisitioned for use by both the Army and the Royal Air Force. The Hall itself escaped the fate of many similar houses that were commandeered to become officers' messes and suffered petty vandalism as a result.

The 1st Parachute Brigade was formed at Hardwick in 1941 and for the remainder of the war the camp on the western side of the park was the depot of the School of Airborne Forces, where volunteers from all ranks went through selection tests and received specialised training. Every airborne participant in the Normandy invasion, including those landed by glider as well as parachutists, went through his initial training at Hardwick. A memorial to the men who trained there stands near the south-west corner of the carpark to the north of the mansion.

After the war the camp was used for a short time to house officers and men of the Polish army who did not wish to return to their own country, and also displaced civilian Poles, mostly young men of below military age, some of whom had been imprisoned in German concentration camps. After the Poles left, some of the buildings were used by the Government as a food store before they once again accommodated refugees from central Europe, this time Hungarians who fled following the rising of 1956. Some of the Hungarians, like some of the Poles a few years earlier, were

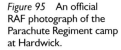

*Figure 95* An official RAF photograph of the Parachute Regiment camp at Hardwick.

allowed to settle in the district if they agreed to work in local collieries, which at the time were having difficulty manning up. After the Hungarians had been rehoused on council estates in local villages, the camp was demolished and little trace of it is visible today.[106] The higher, level ground on the limestone to the east of the mansion was requisitioned by the RAF for a landing strip, which led to the destruction of much of a lime avenue planted by Duchess Evelyn less than 20 years earlier, and also part of a belt of trees planted in the late 19th century to hide Pleasley colliery from sight. The trees were replaced after the war.

## Changes in Farming

Before the more marked changes resulting from the war, the main development in the park in the 1920s and 1930s was the disappearance of the deer herd and the end of the practice of letting the grazing to joist cattle during the summer. By the 1930s local farmers, both tenants and others, had fewer animals and more grass of their own, as a result of the decline of arable farming in the late 19th century. In their place the estate built up a herd. During the war much of the grassland on the better soil of the limestone in the eastern part of the park was ploughed up as part of the campaign to maximise food production.

Until the Second World War, farming on the estate changed very little over a long period, except for a few years during the Great War when there was similar pressure to increase arable cultivation. As we saw in the previous chapter, the number of holdings, their average size and the course of husbandry followed remained much the same from about 1870, when arable began to be put down to permanent grassland, until the 1930s. The survival of a large number of relatively small farms is well illustrated by a map of Ault Hucknall prepared by the Inland Revenue in 1910 following the proposal in the 1909 Budget to tax the capital value of land. This involved the preparation of a detailed survey of every piece of land, and the buildings standing on it, throughout the country, which has rightly been called a 'New Domesday'. The maps showing the farms around Hardwick provide the most detailed picture of the estate since the work of William Senior three centuries before or that the Tithe Commission in the 1840s.

Not only did the size and shape of farms on the estate remain much the same in this period, but so did the villages as a whole. No new farmsteads appear to have been established after the 6th duke's time and there is little sign of renewal of farm buildings. Neither the estate nor (after 1918) the local authorities built any new cottages, and there was virtually no increase in population in the parishes around Hardwick except in the new mining communities.

A good picture of farming during the Second World War is provided by the national survey carried out by the Ministry of Agriculture in 1941. When compared with the earlier annual statistics, this demonstrated that over the previous couple of years there had been more radical change than for at least two

*Figure 96* Farming in Ault Hucknall in 1910, an example of the detailed maps prepared in connection with the land valuation survey carried out under the 1910 Finance Act (the 'New Domesday'). For most parishes they are the fullest such survey since tithe apportionment in the 1840s.

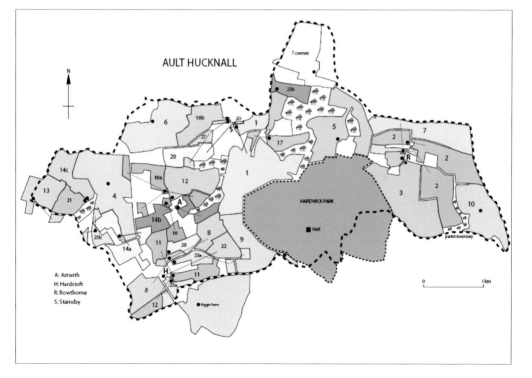

*Figure 97* Holmewood: a tractor owned by the Hardwick Colliery Company.

generations. In 1941 there were 41 holdings of 10 acres of more in Ault Hucknall parish, of which a dozen were smaller than 20 acres. Several of these were being worked part-time by men who had jobs in local collieries or depended on a milk round as their main source of income. The MAF inspector who conducted the survey tended to criticise standards of husbandry on holdings where the tenant had another job, without appreciating that, especially in the case of milk rounds, this was a useful, if not essential, source of cash every week, which small-scale farming was not. The largest farms included four with between 200 and 230 acres and another eight with more than 100 acres. The mean size of holding was 73 acres and the median 56 acres. About forty-five per cent of the area of the parish (some 1,260 acres) was then being ploughed, a considerable increase on the 880 acres of 10 years before. Most of this extra work was being done entirely with horses. There were only five tractors in use on a few of the bigger farms, four Fordsons (the American make imported under Lend-Lease) and one David Brown machine; otherwise the only power available to most farmers (apart from the waterwheel at Stainsby mill, which was still in use) was in the form of small oil engines.[107]

One reason why, until the Second World War, change on the farms around Hardwick was limited compared with elsewhere in north-east Derbyshire was because the land remained part of a great estate. Unlike many of his fellow landowners the 9th duke escaped the worst of the effects of the First World War on such estates. This may have been because of the sheer size of his family's possessions, or the variety of sources of income generated, which included coal royalties as well as rents, or it may have been the outcome of prudent management by the 7th duke and his successors after the heavy expenditure of the 6th duke's time. The estate had also avoided any serious blows from the incidence of death duties, introduced in 1894. Admittedly, Devonshire House was sold and demolished in the early 1920s, and the great conservatory at Chatsworth was taken down because the cost of the coal needed to heat it had risen, but the family made no major disposals. As well as Chatsworth and Hardwick, both Bolton Abbey in Yorkshire and Lismore Castle in what was now the Irish Free State were retained.

The fact that the Hardwick estate remained intact in this period set it apart from a number of its neighbours and meant that the traditional relationship between owner and tenants survived. Among estates in north-east Derbyshire that were broken up by sale in the aftermath of the First World War were two quite close to Hardwick, at Wingerworth, where the Hunloke family had been the principal owners for nearly four centuries, and Sutton Scarsdale, sold by the Arkwrights about a hundred years after they had bought the estate. In neither case was income from coal royalties sufficient to offset the collapse in farm rents, and in both a fine early 18th-century mansion was either demolished or reduced to a ruin soon after the estate was sold. In both cases also many of the farms became owner-occupied, and in Wingerworth quite a lot of farmland was sold for house-building.

At Glapwell the Hallowes family moved away after the death of Brabazon Hallowes in 1892 and let Glapwell Hall until it was sold to the Sheepbridge Company. They in turn let it to one of their directors. The house was eventually demolished by the National Coal Board in the 1950s. Further south the estates of the Turbutt family at Ogston and the Palmer Morewoods at Alfreton remained substantially intact, with resident owners, until after the Second World War, but both were much smaller than the Hardwick estate.

To the north the duke of Portland was still the main owner in Bolsover but the mansion there had long been ruinous and the estate was run entirely from the family's principal seat at Welbeck. The Bathursts' property at Scarcliffe was simply a distant outlier of an estate centred in Gloucestershire. Even before the First World War Hardwick had stood out from its neighbours as the only estate in north-east Derbyshire owned by a major peerage family with a great mansion and park at its heart, although until 1914 it was flanked by a number of middling sized gentry estates. After the war it stood out even more in a much changed landscape.[108]

Figure 98  Wingerworth Hall, photographed in the late 19th century. The mansion was demolished shortly after the Hunloke family estate was broken up by sale in 1920.

Despite the survival of the estate, farming in the area in the 1920s and 1930s was difficult for both landlord and tenant. The late Hugo Read, the former agent to the 11th duke who began his career as the assistant agent in the Chesterfield estate office (from which the Hardwick, Chesterfield and Staveley collections were administered from about 1900), was fond of recounting how he and his principal would sit in the office on rent days in the 1930s, less in the expectation that tenants would come to pay their rent than in the hope that they would not hand in their keys and surrender their tenancy. This story had obviously gained in the telling but equally clearly had a ring of truth to it. There was little capital investment on the estate and, with the family resident at the Hall only for short periods, limited direct employment. Probably only a small proportion of the money paid in rent and coal royalties found its way back into the community.

## A MINING COMMUNITY

One of the most striking features of the Derbyshire and Nottinghamshire coalfield in the first half of the 20th century, a paradox explored repeatedly in the novels of D.H. Lawrence, set a few miles to the south of Hardwick but still concerned with a similar landscape and society, was the way in which traditional landed estates survived alongside the mining communities which had sprung up since the late 19th century. Like most Derbyshire landowners, the Cavendishes did not exploit their own coal, and so did not have the kind of close, paternalistic relationship with miners and their families found, for example, on the Fitzwilliam estate in south Yorkshire. Equally, they could (and did) ensure that the collieries and the villages built to house the miners were kept out of sight of the mansion at Hardwick. But they inevitably had dealings with the colliery companies from whom (until 1938) they received royalties, and could not entirely escape a sense of obligation to the miners living in the villages around Hardwick for whom the inter-war years, punctuated by short-time working and strikes, were so hard. Appeals for funds from churches and chapels continued to be met with donations; fêtes and bazaars were opened and subscriptions were paid to relief funds during the major disputes.[109]

Although the collieries at Holmewood, Williamthorpe and Glapwell all remained open in this period and passed to the National Coal Board in 1947, there were no major developments in the area after sinking at Williamthorpe was completed in 1905. Williamthorpe and, to a lesser extent, Holmewood were modernised in the late 1930s, including a good deal of underground mechanisation, an improved surface layout and

# Life at the Hardwick Park Camp in 1946

After the war the former Airborne Forces camp in Hardwick Park was used for a short time to house some of the large number of Polish soldiers who had fought for the Allies, ended the war in Britain, and did not wish to return to their own country. The camp at Hardwick was established in 1946, before the Polish Resettlement Act of 1947 made longer-term arrangements for such men, and no record of its creation or work appears to survive in The National Archives.

An alternative source for the history of shortlived aspects of post-war reconstruction such as this is the local press. For the Chesterfield area this means the *Derbyshire Times*, then one of the largest circulation county newspapers in England. Within a few weeks of the camp opening, one of their reporters, accompanied by two Polish residents of Chesterfield as interpreters, visited Hardwick and wrote a lengthy and very informative piece about what he found, characteristic of the detailed, straightforward coverage that readers of the *Derbyshire Times* in those days expected and received.

At the time of the visit there were about 200 in the camp, although numbers were expected to rise to 900. As well as soldiers there was a large number of boys in their mid-teens, 'gathered from many corners of the Continent – some who have seen the horrors of German concentration camps, many who are orphans as a result of Nazi butchery', who the soldiers had taken under their wing. At least one had been imprisoned in Auschwitz. It was intended that the boys should be taught English and learn a trade: in practice many went into the pits.

The report concluded on an optimistic note typical of the period. A priest from the Roman Catholic Church of the Holy Family, Chesterfield, had agreed to act as chaplain to the camp, and the Chesterfield branch of the British Legion was to open a canteen for the Poles at Haig House in Glumangate. This evolved into a Polish club which flourished for many years after the men from the camp had either gone home or had settled locally to become a distinctive element in the community, as their descendants remain today.

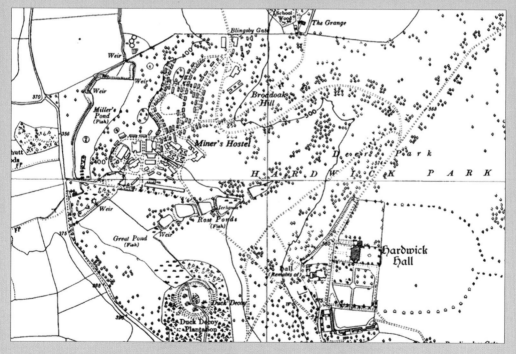

Figure A  *Extract from an Ordnance Survey map of the 1950s showing Hardwick Camp when those living there mostly worked in the mining industry.*

(at Williamthorpe) pit-head baths. In the same period the
Hardwick Colliery Company also took over Ramcroft colliery,
to the north of Heath, which had originally been sunk by the
Markham brothers as an offshoot of their business at Oxcroft,
near Bolsover. Closer to Heath village a small mine was opened
at Doe Lea by Dominic Lavins, a colourful local entrepreneur,
which after 1947 became one of the largest licensed mines in the
Derbyshire coalfield, although it never employed more than a few
dozen men. (Licensed mines were pits vested in the NCB in 1947
but considered too small for the board to work economically;
they were returned to their previous owners who were licensed
to get a certain maximum output each year.) A drift was opened
at Glapwell during the war, known as Bramley Vale, alongside the
existing shafts.[110]

No new houses, nor other buildings, were added to Doe Lea
village once the original layout had been completed c.1900. When
more accommodation was needed for miners working at Glapwell
after the First World War, Sheepbridge used the resources of
the Industrial Housing Association, a public utility company
established by a number of colliery companies in the Yorkshire-
Derbyshire-Nottinghamshire region, to build a completely new
estate of about 150 houses immediately to the south of the pit,
which became known as Bramley Vale. The decision to build the
village was taken in 1923, although in 1927 the local authority
had still not adopted the roads there. The estate added about
500 to the population of Ault Hucknall parish between 1921
and 1931. The houses were larger and better equipped than the

Figure 99   The new
screens at Williamthorpe
colliery, installed in
the late 1930s as part
of a comprehensive
modernisation
programme carried out
by the Hardwick Colliery
Company that enabled
the pit to remain open
until 1970.

*Figure 100* Houses built in the 1920s at Bramley Vale by the Industrial Housing Association for miners at Glapwell colliery.

cottages at Doe Lea, and had gardens, but suffered from being so close to the colliery. When the school at Doe Lea burnt down in 1937 it was not replaced and a new school was built at Bramley Vale, using prefabricated wooden huts of the type adopted by the education committee at a number of places on the coalfield where subsidence was expected. The school provided the only meeting place at Bramley Vale, apart from a pub built at the bottom of Glapwell Hill, since the colliery institute remained at Doe Lea.[111]

The Hardwick Colliery Company did not subscribe to the Industrial Housing Association, nor did it continue building on its own account after the First World War. When additional houses were needed at Holmewood in the 1920s they were built (to the west of the original village) by Chesterfield rural district council. Designed in what was intended to be a homely vernacular style and built of warm, red brick with tiled roofs, laid out in short rows of varying length with gardens, they represented a genuine attempt, like the efforts of the IHA at Bramley Vale, to provide miners with better houses than had been built on the coalfield before 1914. Above all, they had running water and WCs, although not all were built with bathrooms. The new estate lay just inside North Wingfield parish and thus did not increase the population of Heath, which remained around 2,000 in the inter-war period. The colliery company made some attempt to improve the older cottages in the 1930s, for example by installing WCs in place of the earth middens, but as Bas Barker, who was born in the village in 1910 and later became well known as one of the few prominent trade union officers in the Chesterfield area not from the mining industry, remarked in his memoirs, Holmewood seemed to his mother like the last place God made. As he himself said:

You could never say it was a bright place because the smoke,
steam and grime from the colliery and coke ovens hung over
the village like a dull, dark, dank smog. The houses were rows of
terraces owned by the colliery and generally on unmade streets.
On a dark damp day it was as grey as the life of the people who
lived there.[112]

Better houses could not transform Holmewood, any more
than the building of Bramley Vale could improve the quality
of life in the older Sheepbridge cottages at Doe Lea. Both
Holmewood and Doe Lea suffered, socially and economically,
from being dependent on a single employer and slightly isolated
from older communities or from local towns. Glapwell station,
which had provided Doe Lea and Bramley Vale with a limited
passenger service to Chesterfield and Mansfield, closed in 1930.
By then East Midland were running buses between the two towns
through both villages. This offered the chance of a trip to the
shops or the cinema: neither village had anything in the way of
commercial entertainment or any shops apart from a general
store and post office. Holmewood, which had a station on the
former Great Central line with trains to Chesterfield, Sheffield
and Nottingham, began to be served by Chesterfield Corporation
buses in the same period. This enabled some of the women in the
village, where there was virtually no female employment other
than a few shops, to travel to work, for example at Robinson's in
Chesterfield, or as far afield as the lace factories in Nottingham,

*Figure 101* Hardwick
colliery at Holmewood,
viewed from the
north, showing the
layout of the colliery
after modernisation
in the 1930s.

*Figure 102* A flower show held by the Miners' Welfare Association at Holmewood in the 1950s or early 1960s.

but low wages meant that after fares had been paid net earnings were modest. Some women did outwork for Nottingham firms.

Holmewood, unlike Doe Lea or Bramley Vale, was just big enough for a cinema to be opened there in the 1920s, but otherwise the colliery institute and the pubs provided the only social outlets in the village and catered mainly for the men of the community. For many of the women such social life as they enjoyed probably focused more on St Alban's mission church or one of the two Methodist chapels in the village. Regular reports in the local press show that the institute remained at the heart of the community. It was here that the men could play darts, dominoes and snooker, both socially and competitively against other pit teams. The institute also served as the headquarters of the village cricket and football teams. Other activities that were traditionally strong in mining villages included keeping racing pigeons and gardening. Although even the newer houses in Holmewood and Bramley Vale had only small gardens of their own (and the older terraces had none), mining companies were generous in providing allotments as part of their housing schemes. Not only did this enable families to grow some of their own vegetables, but it also encouraged the formation of horticultural clubs, which usually held annual shows every autumn.[113]

Before the Second World War most children from Holmewood or Heath spent their entire school career at either the big block of county council schools midway between the two villages; those from Doe Lea and Bramley Vale went to either the school at Doe Lea or its successor at Bramley Vale; and children from the farming villages near Hardwick went to the school at Stainsby. A handful won places at the secondary schools in Chesterfield, which was easiest of access by bus or train from the area; a few may have attended the central school at Shirebrook or the new grammar school opened at Tupton Hall in the mid-1930s.

## AFTER THE WAR

The death in 1950, aged only 55, of the 10th duke of Devonshire proved to be a marked turning point in the history of both the Cavendish family and their estates. The title passed to the duke's second son, Lord Andrew Cavendish, who had become heir only on the death in Normandy in 1944 of his elder brother William. Lord Andrew himself had served in Italy, where he won the Military Cross. Denied a political career at the highest level which would have been his first choice when he came out of the Army at the end of the war, the new duke and his wife Deborah Mitford, one of the remarkable sextet of daughters of the 2nd Lord Redesdale, faced with great fortitude a quite different world from that in which they had grown up. The first head of his family for centuries not to be appointed lord lieutenant of Derbyshire, the duke had to deal with a strongly Labour county council at home and also a Labour government apparently determined to extract the largest possible sum in death duties from great landowners who had survived thus far. The duke and duchess accepted that one of their two Derbyshire houses would have to be handed to the Treasury in part settlement of death duties. The choice inevitably fell on Hardwick, which had not been a family home since the 17th century. Efforts were concentrated on re-establishing Chatsworth, which had accommodated an evacuated girls' school during the war, not only as a family home, but also as the centre of a still extensive agricultural estate, and a great house open to the public. In all three respects the duke and duchess were outstandingly successful, gradually restoring Chatsworth to much of its former magnificence, retaining as much land as possible, adapting traditional estate management to suit modern farming conditions, and developing Chatsworth as the most important visitor attraction in Derbyshire. At the same time the duke and duchess, as well as being universally respected and admired in Derbyshire, became two of the best known members of the peerage of their generation.

*Figure 103*  A rare example at Holmewood of a modern monument to the dead of the wars of the 20th century.

### Open to the Public

These changes rather passed the east Derbyshire estate by. Although the duke and duchess maintained the family's traditionally close links with Chesterfield and neighbouring villages, the closure of the estate office in the town in 1950, followed by the transfer of the mansion and park at Hardwick to the Treasury, inevitably weakened the connection with the villages immediately adjoining Hardwick. The Hall itself and the park were handed by the Government to the National Trust, while the Old Hall became a guardianship monument in the care of the Ministry of Works, now English Heritage. The Chatsworth estate retained a considerable acreage of farmland in the area, which had been augmented by the purchase in 1943 from Lord Bathurst of his Scarcliffe estate and of land at Bolsover from the Portland estate two years before. The mansion and park, however, the natural heart of the estate, had gone.[114]

The National Trust opened Hardwick Hall to the public almost at once, although it did not become one of their more heavily visited properties until after the opening of the northern section of the M1 in 1965. The motorway, which here follows the valley of the river Doe Lea, was built along the western edge of the park, severing it from Stainsby village. The mansion is easily visible from the motorway and signs at junction 29 encourage visitors to leave the motorway for Hardwick and also for Bolsover Castle and Chatsworth. As at all their properties, the Trust's policy at Hardwick has been simply to present the house and its contents in a straightforward way: there is neither the scope nor the wish to develop ancillary attractions, as at Chatsworth or some of the other great houses in the region opened privately. In any case, unlike Chatsworth, the Hall is no longer the centre of a large working estate. Development has been largely limited to the opening of the former estate corn mill at Stainsby to the public and the restoration of the western side of the park, including the fishponds. This area was designated as a countryside park under the Countryside Act of 1968, and new footpaths and better facilities for anglers installed, together, more recently, with a visitor centre.

At the same time English Heritage, as custodians of the Old Hall, have consolidated the structure, making it possible for the first time for visitors to walk through the ruins. The National Trust have also devoted very large resources to repairing and renewing the stonework of the New Hall, a task made easier since it ceased to be attacked by pollution from local collieries. The juxtaposition of the two houses remains an oddity, as it has been since the New Hall was completed in the 1590s and the Old Hall left standing. Just as visitors in the 17th century may have wondered why Bess did not take down the old building to improve the setting of the new house, so visitors today can

(unusually, if not uniquely) compare the different approaches
to the conservation of two great houses adopted by Britain's two
leading practitioners in the field.

The work of both organisations, English Heritage and the
National Trust, combined with the greater accessibility of the
district since the opening of the M1, has led to an increase in the
number of visitors to Hardwick, but cannot be said to have made
this part of north-east Derbyshire a major tourist destination.
The vast majority of visitors to Hardwick probably come to the
area just for the day, either from home or as part of a short break
in the Peak District or possibly Sherwood Forest. They may also
go to Bolsover Castle while they are in the area, but probably
few stay overnight in the immediate vicinity. This means that
the amount of money visitors spend locally is less than it would
be if there was more to keep them in the area for longer. The
parishes around Hardwick, whilst forming a pleasant backdrop
to the mansion and park, do not offer especially interesting
walking country and the rural areas are in any case interspersed
with former mining villages and modern industrial estates. This
is in marked contrast to either the Peak District to the west or
Sherwood to the east, where it is possible to walk through ancient
woodland unaware that this was quite recently (albeit briefly) a
major coalfield.

The appearance of the landscape today around Hardwick,
although in part an inheritance from the more distant past, is
mainly the result of four changes since the Second World War:
the opening of the M1, the end of large-scale coalmining, the
break-up of the traditional estate centred on Hardwick Hall, and
the restructuring of farming, especially on the coal measures. All
are interrelated, and the course each has taken is either wholly the
result of public policy (as in the case of the M1) or has been greatly
influenced by the actions of central and local government. This
is in contrast to the way in which changes occurred (or did not
occur) in the area in the 19th century and before, which were the
result of decisions by private individuals or corporations, subject to
only slight control from outside.

## Post-War Reconstruction

The immediate post-war years were a period of optimism in the
North Derbyshire coalfield, as they were everywhere. The Ministry
of Agriculture remained a powerful advocate for the farming
industry, determined to keep every acre possible in production,
and the industry prospered, even on the heavy clay soils of the
Derbyshire coalfield and even when organised in relatively small

units. The Ministry of Fuel and Power was equally adamant that every ton of coal was needed, even from ageing pits like Holmewood and Williamthorpe, much of whose output after 1957 went to a huge new carbonisation plant opened that year alongside the Midland main line at Wingerworth. The Ministry of Housing and Local Government was determined to improve working-class housing, not least in the coalfields, and saw the district councils as their main allies in this campaign. A new estate was built by Chesterfield rural district council at Holmewood, to the west of Slack Lane north of the older village, while at Glapwell virtually a new community was laid out south of the main Mansfield Road by Blackwell rural district council, which had built a single street of houses near the Hall in the 1930s. To the east of Hardwick the Blackwell council carried out another large scheme at Shirebrook, closing the gap which had previously existed between the older village, itself largely the product of extremely rapid growth in the 1900s following the opening of a colliery there, and the railway settlement at Langwith Junction. Neither authority did much building in the farming villages in the area, where the existing housing stock, much of it originally built by the Cavendish estate, was deemed adequate in terms of quantity. Efforts were instead concentrated on requiring private landlords to install running water and make other improvements.

*Figure 104*  Part of the large local authority estate at Glapwell, begun in the late 1940s, which greatly extended the built-up area and transformed the social structure of the village.

The last piece in the jigsaw of post-war reconstruction was the work of the county education committee, which in 1960 opened

*Figure 105*  Pamela
Kettle, seated at her
desk as headmistress
of Heath Girls' School
in the early 1950s. Mrs
Kettle, who remained at
Heath after secondary
reorganisation as head
of the junior school, was
an outstanding teacher,
Churchwoman and local
historian. She also served
for many years as an
officer in the Territorial
WRAC. Generations
of children from a very
poor community who
had few advantages in
life benefited from the
example she set.

a new mixed secondary school at the northern end of the old
village of Heath. This replaced two small boys' and girls' schools
set up immediately after the war in the older buildings near
Holmewood, which henceforth were used solely for infants and
juniors. The extra space at Holmewood in turn made it possible
to close the old board school at Stainsby, leaving Bramley Vale
as the only primary school in Ault Hucknall parish itself. The
building at Stainsby then became a music and drama centre,
serving schools throughout north-east Derbyshire, with a former
actor as warden living in the headmaster's house. This was an
imaginative, if shortlived, venture which flourished for a few
years in the 1960s and 1970s.

## AFTER COAL

By the early 1970s the confidence of the post-war years was ebbing
away from places like Holmewood, where the pit closed in 1968,
to be followed two years later by Williamthorpe. The former
Clay Cross Company collieries in the district also closed, as did
Grassmoor, another of the pits which had latterly supplied coal to
the carbonisation plant at Avenue. Glapwell, one of the older pits
sunk to the Top Hard coal in the late 19th century, closed in 1974.
Although these closures were a blow to the villages adjoining the
pits, they did not immediately lead to large-scale unemployment.
While older men left the industry, younger miners could transfer
to the longer-life pits in the North Derbyshire coalfield, such as
Markham and Bolsover, if they were prepared to travel further than
their fathers had done. There were also still plenty of jobs in the
Chesterfield engineering industry at this time. The real problems
only set in some years later, after the strike of 1984-5, when mining

in the district ran down more quickly than had been planned before the dispute, and by which time other industry in the area was also in decline.

In principle, north-east Derbyshire was better placed to deal with the aftermath of colliery closures than more isolated coalfields, thanks to the M1. The local authorities were not slow to grasp the significance of the coming of the motorway and its impact on the economic geography of the area. In the last few years of its life Blackwell rural district council, serving the area to the south of Hardwick, tried to encourage firms to move to its new industrial estates developed on former colliery sites close to junction 28 of the motorway. This work was taken over after local government reorganisation in 1974 by the larger Bolsover district council, which adopted a similar policy elsewhere in its area at junction 30 and in Bolsover itself, although in that case without the advantage (until 2008) of a motorway junction.[115]

The position around junction 29, where the main Chesterfield-Mansfield road crossed the motorway close to the boundary between Bolsover district to the east and North East Derbyshire to the west, was slightly different. Although the motorway here runs very close to the village of Doe Lea and within a couple of miles of Bramley Vale and Holmewood, the only collieries immediately adjacent to the junction were the small licensed mine (Dominic's) and Ramcroft. There was therefore no large acreage of derelict land which could be cleared and new factories built alongside the motorway, but instead (with the exception of Doe Lea village) a rural landscape of high quality on the edge of the park surrounding Hardwick Hall. This could not be released for either opencast coal mining or industrial development in a district where there was plenty of more suitable land.

New factory estates were laid out on the colliery sites at Holmewood, Williamthorpe and Glapwell after the pits closed. At the same time the spoil tips were reprofiled and planted with grass and trees, and at Williamthorpe a nature reserve, with large fishing ponds, was created at the northern end of the colliery site. Much of the branch railway network which served Williamthorpe, Holmewood and other collieries was made into a footpath (open also to cyclists and horse riders) named the Five Pits Trail. Parts of the line between Bolsover and Pleasley through Glapwell were similarly converted to become the Stockley Trail.

When the motorway was opened, the Chesterfield-Mansfield road was realigned on both approaches to junction 29, bypassing Doe Lea. A few years later the opportunity was taken to improve road access from the motorway to the industrial estates at Holmewood and Williamthorpe using land that became available when the

Great Central line through Heath closed in 1963. A more ambitious scheme was the building of a dual carriageway between junction 29 and Chesterfield, also using parts of the Great Central formation between Heath and Hasland, which replaced the old Mansfield road and took traffic away from Heath village. This reorganisation of the road layout around the junction was not accompanied by new building. Whereas at both junction 28 and later junction 30, large new hotels were opened close to the motorway, all that happened at Heath was that some cottages said to have been built for miners at Ramcroft colliery were converted into a small hotel.

Although the motorway may have encouraged the development of new industrial estates close to junction 29, it did not save the villages in the area from suffering the damage caused by pit closures everywhere. None of the new employers could provide jobs on the scale the collieries had done until the 1960s. Some mainly employed women, whereas it was large numbers of men who lost their jobs as mining contracted. Others were distribution companies, easily attracted to sites near motorway junctions, which occupy large units in which very few people, men or women, are needed. Even when combined with more travel to work in other areas, the building of the new estates could not stop Holmewood and Doe Lea from declining badly in the last quarter of the 20th century. With high unemployment came a decline in retail and other services.

*Figure 106* A monument marking the site of Glapwell colliery, and the associated drift mine, Bramley Vale which uses the familiar device of colliery winding sheaves.

*Figure 107* Houses built by Chesterfield rural district council at Holmewood in the 1920s, which marked a great improvement on the earlier cottages put up by the Wingerworth Coal Company.

## The Local Villages

The poor appearance of both villages was aggravated by a lack of home ownership. After the transfer of the NCB's housing stock to local authorities, which began in the 1960s, the vast majority of families lived in council houses and, given the poverty of the area, few had the means to become owner-occupiers when the Conservative government gave them the chance after 1979. There was in any case no tradition of owner-occupation in the North Derbyshire coalfield, where a high proportion of housing had always been provided by employers. This meant that there was no steady improvement of the housing stock as people bought at a discount, modernised and moved on, and no incentive for private developers to build better houses for people to move on to. Despite the best efforts of the local authorities, Holmewood at the end of the 20th century was a deeply deprived one-class community characterised by poor housing, poor services and poor health, all problems ultimately stemming from the loss of the type of employment that called the village into existence in the first place.

The villages near Hardwick to the east of junction 29 form something of a contrast with Holmewood and with each other. At Doe Lea there was arguably a strong case for completely demolishing the village. It was isolated, had few services and had never expanded beyond its original limits, since later housing had been built at Bramley Vale and Glapwell, whereas Holmewood had continued to grow up to the 1950s and was a much bigger village. In 1973, shortly before Glapwell colliery closed, Blackwell rural district council demolished West Street at Doe Lea, and about ten years later their successors, Bolsover district council, cleared all but a couple of cottages on East Street. New local authority houses were built on both roads in the late 1970s. Further regeneration did not follow for some years, until in 2007 a major private housing development named 'The Brambles' began close to the site of the old village. This effectively created a new settlement, conveniently near the motorway junction, but lacking any services apart from a well-equipped community centre created out of the old colliery institute. The Anglican mission church closed in 1991 and was later demolished; the Primitive Methodist chapel has also long been disused and derelict. Regeneration was much less extensive at Bramley Vale, although the school has remained open, some of the housing stock has been improved after sales to sitting tenants, and a few new houses have been built since the turn of the century.[116]

The biggest contrast, however, and the only village in this group that can be described as a genuinely mixed community, is Glapwell itself. Here the older farms and cottages along the main road were augmented by some private building on Glapwell Hill between the First and Second World Wars, and a small council estate near the Hall. After the war a much larger local authority scheme was built south of the main road, which included a central open space on which various community buildings were erected. Despite the loss of local employment at the colliery, this estate has remained just as well cared for as the housing elsewhere in the village. This has in turn been upgraded in recent years, as farmworkers' cottages have been bought and extended by incomers and some larger private houses have been built. At the same time, farming has survived in the village, which has retained some retail and other services, including a pub with a good local and passing trade, although it has never had its own school. The village may still lack the bypass for which the parish council has campaigned for years, but in no sense does the main road divide Glapwell into two, either socially or otherwise. The strong sense of community is immediately apparent to the visitor through such diverse indicators as the tidiness of the streets, gardens and open spaces throughout the village, and the success of the local cricket and football teams, which have evolved from traditional pit sides into well supported clubs punching above their weight in their respective leagues.[117]

A similar upgrading has also occurred in the housing stock of the other villages around Hardwick which were unaffected by the growth of the coal industry, although by a rather different route and achieved, as in much of rural England, at the expense of a narrowing of the social structure.

## Farms and Cottages

When the mansion and park at Hardwick passed to the Treasury in partial settlement of death duties following the death of the 10th duke, the Chatsworth estate retained most of the tenanted farms and cottages. Indeed, the estate still owns a considerable acreage of agricultural land in the parishes around Hardwick let to tenant farmers and some private houses, particularly in Heath. There was a steady process of amalgamation of farms, especially on the coal measures, where holdings had traditionally been smaller than on the limestone, and this made a number of farmhouses and their buildings redundant. All the land around Astwith is today farmed as a single holding, whereas there were half a dozen farmers in the village during and after the Second World War. Several farmers, as much because of advancing years as through any worries concerning what the future held, took the opportunity to retire or move when the National Trust took over the Hall, and the number of those remaining has fallen steadily over the last 50 years.

At the same time, the farms employed fewer men, and those who stayed on the land were less likely to live in traditional tied cottages and more likely to own their own homes or be tenants of the local authority. The nature of farming also changed. Oats largely disappeared once tractors replaced horses, and by the end of the 20th century barley had become the main grain crop. At Ault Hucknall in 1960 there were 311 acres of oats, 298 acres of barley and 417 acres of wheat, whereas in 1987 only 35 acres of oats were being grown, compared with 652 acres of wheat and no less than 952 acres of barley. Kale gradually replaced the various roots as a fodder crop and, after the United Kingdom joined the Common Market and thus the farming industry became subject to the Common Agricultural Policy, new 'industrial' crops such as oilseed rape and linseed began to be grown on a large scale.[118]

The changes in farm size and employment created a pool of surplus houses, farm buildings and cottages which the Chatsworth estate gradually sold. Similarly, small pieces of land within the existing built-up area in some of the villages, particularly Heath and Upper Langwith, were sold with planning permission for housing, although there was no large-scale development of private housing in any of the villages around Hardwick. In general, planning control, exercised until 1974 by the county council, rather than the districts, ensured that the new houses, like the extensions added to many of the older cottages, fitted into the existing street picture in the villages affected. Materials, elevations and densities were carefully controlled, with only occasional lapses, notably one very badly designed estate at Heath, built in the grounds of the Victorian parsonage. The only other residential development of any size was built in the early 1990s on the site of the secondary school in Heath, which closed barely 30 years after it was opened. Heath, by some way the largest of the traditional farming villages on the estate, benefited considerably in this period not only from the opening of the motorway but also the building of the new roads from junction 29 to Holmewood and Chesterfield, which effectively removed through-traffic from the main street. All the villages gained from the closure of the collieries, which reduced the amount of airborne pollution.

## Social and Economic Life Today

The sale of older houses and the building of new ones, although on a limited scale, changed the social structure of the district. Until the Second World War, outside the mining villages, most people who lived near Hardwick Hall were tenants of the estate, whether they were farmers, farm labourers, tradesmen (such as blacksmiths or wheelwrights), shopkeepers or licensees. A smaller number of families depended more directly on the estate as indoor or outdoor servants at the Hall itself. Almost the only other residents in the villages on the estate were the clergy (holding livings of which the duke of Devonshire was patron), schoolteachers and perhaps a doctor. Otherwise there was no middle class or lower middle class and almost everyone worked close to where they lived, most of them on the land. This traditional structure was largely unaffected by the coming of large-scale mining, since this led to the building of new, separate communities, not (as for example at Tibshelf or Shirebrook elsewhere in the district) the addition of new housing to an old village.

Nor did the coming of the railway lead to the building of what contemporaries called 'villa estates' near the stations, from which business and professional men could commute daily to work in a nearby town, because the few railways that did penetrate the area offered a very poor passenger service. Nowhere around Chesterfield, in fact, developed in this way in the late 19th century, whereas villages close to Sheffield, such as Dore and Totley, and later Grindleford and Hathersage, were transformed by the railway. Similarly, because the Hardwick estate remained intact during the period of the great sales after the First World War, no land was released for building in the 1920s and 1930s, as happened at Wingerworth after the break-up of the Hunloke estate. In any case, the villages near Hardwick were too poorly served by buses to be

*Figure 108*  Vicarage Close, Heath. Private houses built on the site of the Victorian vicarage.

attractive to speculative builders until car ownership became more general after the Second World War. The same was true of the small village near the mansion at Sutton Scarsdale, where the estate was broken up by sale at the same time as Wingerworth, but few new houses were built because it was too far from Chesterfield.

Only from the 1960s did Heath, Stainsby, Astwith, Hardstoft and Rowthorne begin to be affected by the process, which has transformed so much of rural England in the last 50 years, whereby most of those who live in the countryside have no connection with the land but travel daily to work elsewhere. In the case of the villages around Hardwick the process was initiated by the sale of buildings and land by the estate but accelerated by the opening of the M1. Once again junction 29 played a pivotal role, in that it lay within a few minutes' drive of the villages near Hardwick and provided access to Sheffield, Nottingham and further afield. Just as the motorway enabled far more people to visit Hardwick Hall on day trips, so it made long-distance commuting from the neighbouring villages practicable, whereas previously the slowness of the older main roads serving the area (and the distance from the nearest main-line station at Chesterfield) had made such journeys impossible. The villages were also attractive places to live for senior staff employed at the new factories that grew up around junction 28 on the motorway or elsewhere in the district, certainly when compared with the former mining villages in the area.

Much of the distinctive character of the area today results directly from its history as part of a great estate that survived until the middle of the 20th century. As well as the striking views of Hardwick Hall that can be seen on the skyline from most directions, both the villages and the farmland retain the neat and tidy appearance associated with communities controlled by a single owner, which has been enhanced by the careful upgrading of the individual buildings as they have passed into private hands. This is perhaps especially true of the area to the east of the Hall, around Rowthorne, which has been spared the intrusion of the motorway and the constant drone of traffic noise that comes with it. All the villages benefit from being close to the amenities of Hardwick Park, which provides a variety of walks in an area that lacks either the moorland or woodland that can be found elsewhere in north Derbyshire and north Nottinghamshire.

The proximity of the motorway junction and the charm of the villages appear to have outweighed their disadvantages. Perhaps the most obvious was the lack of a local authority primary school of the sort favoured by the rural middle class. The late Victorian schoolroom on the top of the hill at Stainsby, which would have been ideal for this purpose, closed just before the influx of new families began; the older Church school in Heath had by then long been given up. This left only the wooden huts at Bramley Vale or the forbidding red-brick blocks at Holmewood, both with predominantly working-class intakes, as the alternative to a daily drive to the nearest private schools in Chesterfield. As a recent

*Figure 109* Junction 29 of the M1, which since it opened in 1965 has become a nodal point for the local economy.

*Figure 110* The *Shoulder of Mutton*, Hardstoft. A simple wayside inn transformed in the late 20th century into a popular pub-restaurant.

inspection noted, although the school at Holmewood is called Heath primary school, virtually no children from Heath attend. Similarly, the nearest local authority secondary schools likely to find favour with the new arrivals were in Chesterfield. A further disadvantage for older school children was the lack of any sort of commercial entertainment accessible other than by car. Daily driving was also essential for shopping. For all but the most basic essentials, shopping meant going into Chesterfield or Mansfield.

On the other hand, the area was better provided with pubs serving meals. Quite early in the transformation of the district, when an evening of prawn cocktail, chicken and chips and Black Forest gateau was still viewed as something of a culinary adventure in north-east Derbyshire, the *Shoulder of Mutton* at Hardstoft acquired local fame as a smart place to eat out. The *Shoulder*'s early lead was soon challenged by the *Hardwick Inn*, which built up a reputation for serving excellent food in an attractive setting that combines elements of the pub's Jacobean origins with the atmosphere of a Victorian country inn created by the 6th duke's careful rebuilding. Both continue to flourish.

Between about 1960 and the end of the 20th century the social and economic structure of the area around Hardwick changed radically in two quite different ways. The colliery villages went into decline as the industry which had called them into existence and sustained them for about three generations came to an end, leaving them with severe problems that may take longer to solve than they did to create. At the same time a traditional rural estate,

while not disappearing entirely, shrank in size and influence. In
this case the villages on the estate, instead of declining, found
a new role as homes for middle-class commuters and thus
the houses were rejuvenated and extended, whereas the older
housing in the mining villages was demolished and the surviving
stock suffered neglect. Although great efforts have been made
to regenerate the local economy since the end of coal mining,
and to improve the physical environment of the former mining
communities in the area, the contrast between, say, Holmewood
and Heath remains in the early 21st century as stark as it was at
the beginning of the 20th century when Holmewood was built.
Both villages have changed a great deal in appearance, social
structure and relative prosperity, but to travel from one to the
other is to see, within the space of a few minutes, the way in which
the fortunes of different communities in the North Derbyshire
coalfield, both on the Hardwick estate and elsewhere, have varied
so dramatically within a short period of time.

# Endnotes

The following abbreviations are used throughout the endnotes:

DAJ         *Derbyshire Archaeological Journal* (and its predecessor, the *Journal of the Derbyshire Archaeological and Natural History Society*)

Oxford DNB  *Oxford Dictionary of National Biography*

DRS         Derbyshire Record Society

## CHAPTER 2 The Making of a Great Estate, pp.11-39

1  The most reliable biography of Bess remains D.N. Durant, *Bess of Hardwick: Portrait of an Elizabethan Dynast* (1977), which, except as indicated, has been drawn on in this chapter.

2  This section summarises the conclusions of P. Riden, 'The Hardwicks of Hardwick Hall in the fifteenth and sixteenth centuries', *DAJ* (2010), 130.

3  *Derbyshire Visitation Pedigrees 1569 and 1611* (1895).

4  P. Riden, 'The Hardwicks', corrects a number of errors in previous accounts of Bess's early life.

5  P. Riden, 'Sir William Cavendish: Tudor civil servant and founder of a dynasty', *DAJ* (2009), 109 provides a revised view of Cavendish's career.

6  P. Riden, 'Bess of Hardwick and the St Loe inheritance' in P. Riden and D.G. Edwards (eds), *Essays in Derbyshire History presented to Gladwyn Turbutt*, DRS, 30 (2006), provides a new account of Bess's third marriage.

7  Durant, *Bess*, remains the best account of Bess's fourth marriage and final widowhood; for Shrewsbury see also *Oxford DNB*.

8  Sheffield Archives, ACM S113-S118.

9  L. Worsley, *Hardwick Old Hall* (1998); M. Girouard, *Robert Smythson and the Architecture of the Elizabethan Era* (1966), ch. 4 (summarised in successive editions of the National Trust guide to Hardwick written by Girouard); D.N. Durant and P. Riden (eds), *The Building of Hardwick Hall. Part 1. The Old Hall, 1587-91*, DRS, 4 (1980).

10  G.R. Batho, 'Gilbert Talbot, seventh earl of Shrewsbury (1553-1616): the "Great and Glorious Earl"?', *DAJ*, 93 (1973), 23-32; A.S. Turberville, *A History of Welbeck Abbey and its Owners* (1938), vol. I; P. Riden and D. Fowkes, *Bolsover: Castle, Town and Colliery* (2008), ch. 5.

11    For descriptions of the New Hall, with plans, see Girouard,
      *Robert Smythson*, 120-30; D.N. Durant and P. Riden, *The Building
      of Hardwick Hall. Part 2. The New Hall, 1591-98*, DRS, 9 (1984).

12    P. Kettle, *Oldcotes: The Last Mansion built by Bess of Hardwick*
      (2000).

13    These purchases have been traced from deeds and rentals at
      Chatsworth.

14    For Bess's final years and death see Durant, *Bess*, chapters 13
      and 14; for the contents of the two houses at Hardwick see *Of
      Household Stuff: The 1601 Inventories of Bess of Hardwick* (2001);
      there are copies of Bess's will at Chatsworth.

15    Purchases traced from deeds and rentals at Chatsworth.

16    The 1st earl's career can be traced from his household accounts
      at Chatsworth, and the development of his estate from deeds and
      rentals in the Devonshire Collection. For Arbella and the peerage
      of 1605 see Durant, *Bess*, 219; for the 2nd earl's public life see
      *History of Parliament. Commons. 1558-1603*; *Oxford DNB*.

17    This analysis of the origins of the Cavendish estate has been
      made by identifying (as far as is possible) the purchaser of each
      component of the estate as it existed in 1625 (the last complete
      year of the 1st earl's life) and valuing it using the earl's rental for
      that year.

### CHAPTER 3 Hardwick in the Seventeenth Century, pp.41-69

18    For the 1st earl's life after Bess's death, the main sources are his
      household accounts at Chatsworth.

19    For inventories of the 1st and 2nd earl's personal estate, the
      Act of 1628 and other documents, see Devonshire Collection,
      Hardwick MS 87; for the family generally in the 17th century see
      F. Bickley, *The Cavendish Family* (1911), ch.3, and J. Pearson, *The
      Serpent and the Stag* (1983), ch.4.

20    For Countess Christian see *Oxford DNB*; for her estate
      management during the minority of the 3rd earl see rentals and
      accounts at Chatsworth.

21    For the 3rd earl, in addition to Bickley, *Cavendish Family*, and
      Pearson, *The Stag and the Serpent*, see *Oxford DNB*; for the
      Derbyshire estates during the Civil War and Interregnum see the
      Derbyshire receiver's accounts at Chatsworth; for the 3rd earl at
      Rouen see A. Tinniswood, *The Verneys* (2007), 225.

22    Devonshire Collection, 3rd earl's receiver's accounts, lease book
      and related documents; and deeds relating to the Hartington and
      Staveley purchases.

23    There is a good account of the 1st duke in *Oxford DNB*; for day-
      to-day estate administration in the 1690s see the letters of Aaron
      Kinton, his London receiver, at Chatsworth.

24    The summary of estate organisation given here has been

reconstructed from the receivers' accounts and subsidiary
accounting records at Chatsworth.

25 The account that follows is based on these records.

26 See P. Riden, *Tudor and Stuart Chesterfield* (1984), ch.5 for local
lead merchants and the trade of the town generally.

27 P. Riden, 'The charcoal iron industry in the East Midlands 1580-
1780', *DAJ*, 111 (1991), 64-84; P. Riden (ed.), *George Sitwell's
Letterbook 1662-66*, DRS, 10 (1985).

28 Riden and Fowkes, *Bolsover*, 43-4.

29 F. Brodhurst, 'Extracts from a book of accounts of a lady's
waiting woman for moneys disbursed in cloathes etc. for Elizth.
Countess of Devonshire and ffamily. Beginning 1656 ending
1662', *DAJ*, 27 (1905), prints entries from this volume, which is
now Hardwick MS 15a at Chatsworth.

30 D. and S. Lysons, *Magna Britannia. V. Derbyshire* (1817), 34n.,
quoting John Jones, *The Benefits of the Baths of Buxton* (1572)
(spelling modernised).

31 The following account is based on D.V. Fowkes and G.R. Potter
(eds), *William Senior's Survey of the Estates of the First and Second
Earls of Devonshire c.1600-28*, DRS, 13 (1988), the accompanying
atlas at Chatsworth, and rentals, leases, lease books and a court
book for Stainsby, also at Chatsworth.

32 V.S. Doe, 'The common fields of Beeley in the seventeenth century',
*DAJ*, 93 (1973), 45-54; DRO, Q/RI 5, 217, Q/RI 62, Q/RI 89.

33 Account based on sampling wills and inventories for Ault
Hucknall in Lichfield Record Office, B/C/11.

34 P. Kettle, *The Hardwick Inn* (1991); D.G. Edwards (ed.),
*Derbyshire Wills proved in the Prerogative Court of Canterbury
1575-1601*, DRS, 31(2003); R. Sheppard, 'The Evidence for
Changes to Farm Buildings on the Devonshire Estate in the
Parish of Ault Hucknall, Derbyshire, during the mid-late 19th
century' (2008).

## CHAPTER 4 Hardwick and Chatsworth in 1700, pp.71-9

35 This conclusion is based on a close study of all the 17th-century
receivers' accounts at Chatsworth and other estate records.

36 Devonshire Collection, James Whildon's accounts and Aaron
Kinton's letters.

37 For the rebuilding of Chatsworth see (in addition to surviving
accounts in the Devonshire Collection) F. Thompson, *A History
of Chatsworth* (1949); J. Barnatt and T. Williamson, *Chatsworth:
A Landscape History* (2005), ch.3.

38 For the 3rd earl's funeral see Pearson, *The Stag and the Serpent*, 58.

39 B. Cowell, 'Hardwick Hall in the eighteenth century', *Georgian
Group Journal*, 16 (2008), 44; M. Girouard, *Hardwick Hall* (1989
edn), 38-9.

CHAPTER 5 Georgian Hardwick, pp.81-107

40   Barnatt and Williamson, *Chatsworth*, ch.4.
41   Pearson, *The Stag and the Serpent*, chs 6-10, provides a general
     account of the family and its estates in the 18th century.
42   Except as indicated, the following is based on the incomplete
     series of receivers' accounts for the 18th century dispersed
     among the AS series at Chatsworth.
43   J. Farey, *A General View of the Agriculture and Minerals of
     Derbyshire* (1811-17), II, 223, provides a good description of
     managing springwoods to produce a regular supply of cordwood
     in the early 19th century; for Staveley ironworks in this period
     see Riden, 'Charcoal iron industry', 71-80.
44   P. Riden (ed.), *Derbyshire Directories 1781-1824*, DRS, 33 (2006),
     3, 53.
45   For the Barkers see J.W. Clay (ed.), *Familiae Minorum Gentium*
     (1894-6), 214; L. Willies, 'The Barker family and the eighteenth-
     century lead business', *DAJ*, 93 (1973), 55-74.
46   B. Cowell, 'Hardwick Hall in the eighteenth century', 47.
47   DRO, Q/RI 62 and 89; 7 & 8 Geo. IV c. iv.
48   D. Fowkes, 'An analysis of the 1795 crop returns for the hundred
     of Scarsdale', *DAJ*, 115 (1995), 151.
49   Farey, *General View*, II, 136, 144-5.
50   J.V. Beckett and J.E. Heath (eds), *Derbyshire Tithe Files 1836-50*,
     DRS, 22 (1995), 1-2, 77-9, 99-100; Farey, *General View*, II, 438.
51   Farey, *General View*, II, 35-6, 390.
52   Devonshire Collection, AS 191, AS 372-373, AS 480, AS 570.
53   Devonshire Collection, AS 1068-1075.
54   Cowell, 'Hardwick Hall in the eighteenth century', on which the
     following is largely based. See also Girouard's 1989 edition of the
     National Trust guide, pp. 39-42.
55   B. Wragg and G. Worsley, *Carr of York* (2000), 35, 153-4.
56   Cowell, 'Hardwick Hall in the eighteenth century', 56; J. Lees-
     Milne, *The Bachelor Duke. William Spencer Cavendish 6th Duke
     of Devonshire 1790-1858* (1991), 14-15.
57   C.B. Andrews, *The Torrington Diaries* (1934-8), II, 30-2; J.
     Pilkington, *A View of the Present State of Derbyshire* (1789),
     II, 345. Byng's equally widely quoted contemporary among
     visitors to Derbyshire, John Bray, author of *Sketch of a Tour into
     Derbyshire and Yorkshire* (1782), did not visit Hardwick.
58   The following paragraphs summarise accounts to be included in
     a forthcoming Derbyshire VCH volume.
59   *A Seventeenth-century Scarsdale Miscellany*, DRS, 20 (1993), 20-1;
     *White's Directory of Derbyshire* (1857), 767-8.
60   Figures derived from *Derbyshire Population Statistics 1563-2001*,
     DRS, forthcoming; Pilkington, *View*, II, 345.
61   Pilkington, *View*, II, 342-52.

62   DRO, D1476/A/PO/1; Farey, *General View*, III, 551.

63   *Report of the Charity Commissioners* (1826), 604-8.

64   J. Beckett et al. (eds), *Visitation Returns from the Archdeaconry of Derby 1718-1824*, DRS, 29 (2003), 119; *Rep. Char. Comm.* (1826).

65   Girouard, *Hardwick Hall*, 89; OS Map, 1:10,560, Derb. XXXI (1920 edn).

66   M.R. Austin (ed.), *The Church in Derbyshire in 1823-4* (Derb. Archaeological Soc. Rec. Ser. 5, 1969-70), 37-8; *Rep. Char. Comm.* (1826), 769-70, 602-8; Beckett (ed.), *Visitation Returns*, 42, 119.

67   J.C. Cox, *Notes on the Churches of Derbyshire* (1875-9), IV, 466-7, 469.

68   M.R. Austin (ed.), *The Church in Derbyshire in 1823-4* (1969-70), 37-8, 102, 173-4.

69   Austin, *Church in Derbyshire*, 44-5; Cox, *Churches of Derbyshire*, I, 94-5; Hardwick collection annual accounts for the years in question.

70   *VCH Derbyshire*, II, 39-40; J.C. Cox, *Three Centuries of Derbyshire Annals*, I (1890), 293, 303, 368; Beckett (ed.), *Visitation Returns*, 42, 116, 119, 125, 164, 175.

71   Cox, *Three Centuries*, I, 289, 293, 303; R. Clark, *Derbyshire Papist Returns 1705-6*, DRS (1983), 2, 14.

## CHAPTER 6 Victorian and Edwardian Hardwick, pp.109-47

72   Except as indicated, this section is based on the annual Hardwick collection accounts at Chatsworth. For the estate as a whole in this period see D. Cannadine, 'The landowner as millionaire: the finances of the dukes of Devonshire *c.*1800-*c.*1926', *Agricultural History Review*, 25 (1977), 77-97.

73   *Second Report of the Commissioners on the Employment of Children etc. in Agriculture* (Parl. Papers 1868-9, [4202-I], XIII), 424.

74   This and the previous paragraphs are based on TNA, MAF 68/236, MAF 68/1832, MAF 68/3506; MAF 32/309/157; DRO, D2360/3/14B.

75   Sheppard, 'Evidence for Changes'; Kettle, *Hardwick Inn*, 55-7.

76   *Second Report etc.* (1868-9), 424.

77   *Second Report etc.* (1868-9), 424.

78   TNA, RG 10/3466; RG 13/3133.

79   TNA, HO 107/2148; RG 11/3439.

80   This section is based on the annual collection accounts.

81   TNA, HO 107/2123; RG 12/2649.

82   National Trust, *A Short Guide to Hardwick Park* (n.d.).

83   See the vouchers to the Hardwick estate account for the years in question.

84   For other work by Rollinson and by Davies & Tew see the index

to the Derbyshire volume of the Buildings of England series; for Lindley's work at Hardwick see Cowell, 'Hardwick Hall in the eighteenth century', 56.

85   Lees-Milne, *Bachelor Duke*, 17-18, 105-6, 164-5, 168, 172, 213-15; V. Markham, *Paxton and the Bachelor Duke* (1935), 292-3, 297-301.

86   Kettle, *Oldcotes*, 83-4, 92-5.

87   Early 19th-century mining in the parish of North Wingfield, to the west of Ault Hucknall, will be treated in a forthcoming volume of Derbyshire VCH.

88   Records of the Wingerworth and Hardwick coal companies in private hands; D.G. Edwards, *A Historical Gazetteer and Bibliography of By-Product Coking Plants in the United Kingdom* (2001), 55.

89   This account of Doe Lea is based on Sheepbridge Company minute books in the DRO, newspaper reports, and the 1901 census enumeration.

90   Riden and Fowkes, *Bolsover*, 101-2.

91   Hardwick Colliery Company Ltd records in private hands.

92   A. Higgins, '*A Hand to Mouth Existence'. Women's Lives in Holmewood before 1950* (n.d. *c.*1993), 23, 27; P. Turner, *A Social History of the Village of Holmewood 1868-1968* (1980), 5.

93   Subsection based, in addition to other sources cited, on the annual collection accounts.

94   *White's Directory of Sheffield* (1852), 557.

95   *White's Directory of Derbyshire* (1857), 758.

96   *Rep. Char. Comm.* (1826), 604-9; *Bagshaw's Directory of Derbyshire* (1846), 649; *White's Directory of Derbyshire* (1857), 754; *Harrod's Directory of Derbyshire* (1860), 369; *Kelly's Directory of Derbyshire* (1895), 259.

97   *White's Directory of Sheffield* (1862), 692; *Harrod's Directory of Derbyshire* (1870), 26.

98   TNA, ED 2/84; M. Finney, *Men of Iron. A History of the Sheepbridge Company* (Chesterfield, 1995), 70-1.

99   TNA, ED 2/84; *Bulmer's Directory of Derbyshire* (1895), 48-9; *Kelly's Directory of Derbyshire* (1899), 36.

100  N. Pevsner and E. Williamson, *Buildings of England. Derbyshire* (1979), 244.

101  M.R. Austin, '*Under the Heavy Clouds'. The Church of England in Derbyshire and Nottinghamshire, 1911-1915* (2004), 188-9.

102  E.M. Tranter (ed.), *The Derbyshire Returns to the 1851 Religious Census* (Derbyshire Record Society, 23, 1995), 37; *White's Directory of Derbyshire* (1857), 678-9; *White's Directory of Sheffield* (1862), 692.

103  *Rep. Char. Comm.* (1826), 604-8, 770, 771.

CHAPTER 7 Hardwick in the Twentieth Century, pp.149-77

104 Except as indicated, this section is based on Girouard, *Hardwick Hall* (1989 edn), 44-6, 86-7.

105 Marchioness Curzon of Kedleston, *Reminiscences* (1955), 149.

106 Local inf.

107 TNA, MAF 32/309/157.

108 Sale cats. for Wingerworth and Sutton Scarsdale in Chesterfield Library; D.G. Edwards, *The Hunlokes of Wingerworth Hall* (1976); G. Turbutt, *A History of Ogston* (1975); details of Glapwell estate taken from forthcoming Derbyshire VCH volume; for the sale of Lord Bathurst's estate in 1943 see T. Warrener, *A History of Nether Langwith, Langwith & Whaley Thorns* (1999), I, 5.

109 For the Fitzwilliam estate see C. Bailey, *Black Diamonds. The Rise and Fall of an English Dynasty* (2007); the Cavendish family's involvement with the community is reflected in the columns of the *Derbyshire Times*, the weekly paper serving Chesterfield and north-east Derbyshire.

110 See booklet in Chesterfield Library describing the modernisation of Williamthorpe and Hardwick Colliery Company records in private hands; typescript history of Doe Lea colliery ('Dominics') in Chesterfield Library; local inf. concerning other pits mentioned.

111 J.T. Walters, *The Building of Twelve Thousand Houses* (1927), pl. 1; DRO, Blackwell RDC minutes.

112 B. Barker, *Free but not Easy* (1989), 1-2; the first four chapters of Barker's memoirs provide an excellent picture of life in Holmewood in the early 20th century.

113 Higgins, *'A Hand to Mouth Existence'*; Turner, *Holmewood*; local inf.

114 Date of purchase of Scarcliffe estate: Warrener, *Langwith & Whaley Thorns*, I, 5; purchase from duke of Portland: inf. from from Welbeck Estates Co.

115 Riden and Fowkes, *Bolsover*, ch.10.

116 Local inf. and local authority minutes.

117 K.G. Jackson, *'Pause to Remember': Glapwell Parish, its origins and progress towards the millennium 2000* (n.d., *c.*1998).

118 TNA, MAF 68/4678, MAF 68/6051; local inf.

# Bibliography

## PARLIAMENTARY PAPERS

*Second Report of the Commissioners on the Employment of Children etc. in Agriculture* (Parl. Papers, 1868-9 [4202-I], XIII)

*Reports of the Commissioners ... to Inquire concerning Charities and Education of the Poor in England and Wales* (Parl. Papers, 1826 (382), XII)

## OTHER PUBLICATIONS

*Derbyshire Visitation Pedigrees 1569 and 1611* (1895)

*Of Household Stuff: The 1601 Inventories of Bess of Hardwick* (Swindon, 2001)

*A Seventeenth-century Scarsdale Miscellany* (Derbyshire Record Society, 20, 1993)

Andrews, C.B. (ed.), *The Torrington Diaries* (London, 1934-8)

Austin, M.R. (ed.), *The Church in Derbyshire in 1823-4* (Derbyshire Archaeological Society Record Series, 5, 1969-70)

Austin, M.R., *'Under the Heavy Clouds': The Church of England in Derbyshire and Nottinghamshire, 1911-1915* (Cardiff, 2004)

*Bagshaw's Directory of Derbyshire* (1846)

Bailey, C., *Black Diamonds: The Rise and Fall of an English Dynasty* (London, 2007)

Barker, B., *Free but not Easy* (Derbyshire County Council, 1989)

Barnatt, J. and Williamson, T., *Chatsworth: A Landscape History* (Oxford, 2005)

Batho, G.R., 'Gilbert Talbot, seventh earl of Shrewsbury (1553-1616): the "Great and Glorious Earl"?', *DAJ*, 93 (1973), 23-32

Beckett, J.V. and Heath, J.E. (eds), *Derbyshire Tithe Files 1836-50* (Derbyshire Record Society, 22, 1995)

Beckett J., Tranter, M. and Bateman, W. (eds), *Visitation Returns from the Archdeaconry of Derby 1718-1824* (Derbyshire Record Society, 29, 2003)

Bickley, F., *The Cavendish Family* (London, 1911)

Brodhurst, F., 'Extracts from a book of accounts of lady's waiting woman for moneys disbursed in cloathes, &c., ffor Elizth. Countess of Devonshire and ffamily. Beginning 1656. Ending 1662', *DAJ*, 27 (1905), 1-10

*Bulmer's Directory of Derbyshire* (Derbyshire, 1895)

Cannadine, D., 'The landowner as millionaire: the finances of the dukes of Devonshire *c*.1800-*c*.1926', *Agricultural History Review*, 25 (1977), 77-97

Clark, R. (ed.), *The Derbyshire Papist Returns of 1705-6* (Derbyshire Record Society, 1983)

Clay, J.W. (ed.), *Familiae Minorum Gentium* (Harleian Society, 37-40, 1894-6)

Cowell, B., 'Hardwick Hall in the eighteenth century', *Georgian Group Journal*, 16 (2008), 44

Cox, J.C., *Notes on the Churches of Derbyshire* (Chesterfield, 1875-9)

Cox, J.C., *Three Centuries of Derbyshire Annals* (Chesterfield, 1890)

Curzon, Grace Elvina, Marchioness Curzon of Kedleston, *Reminiscences* (London, 1955)

Doe, V.S., 'The common fields of Beeley in the seventeenth century', *DAJ*, 93 (1973), 45-54

Durant, D.N., *Bess of Hardwick: Portrait of an Elizabethan Dynast* (London, 1977)

Durant, D.N. and Riden, P. (eds), *The Building of Hardwick Hall. Part 1. The Old Hall, 1587-91* (Derbyshire Record Society, 4, 1980)

Durant, D.N. and Riden, P. (eds), *The Building of Hardwick Hall. Part 2. The New Hall, 1591-98* (Derbyshire Record Society, 9, 1984)

Edwards, D.G., *The Hunlokes of Wingerworth Hall* (Chesterfield, 1976)

Edwards, D.G., *A Historical Gazetteer and Bibliography of By-Product Coking Plants in the United Kingdom* (Cardiff, 2001)

Edwards, D.G. (ed.), *Derbyshire Wills proved in the Prerogative Court of Canterbury 1575-1601* (Derbyshire Record Society, 31, 2003)

Farey, J., *A General View of the Agriculture and Minerals of Derbyshire* (1811-17)

Finney, M., *Men of Iron: A History of the Sheepbridge Company* (Chesterfield, 1995)

Fowkes, D., 'An analysis of the 1795 crop returns for the hundred of Scarsdale', *DAJ*, 115 (1995), 149-53

Fowkes, D.V. and Potter, G.R. (eds), *William Senior's Survey of the Estates of the First and Second Earl of Devonshire c.1600-28* (Derbyshire Record Society, 13, 1988)

Girouard, M., *Robert Smythson and the Architecture of the Elizabethan Era* (London, 1966)

Girouard, M., *Hardwick Hall* (Swindon, 1989 edn)

*Harrod's Directory of Derbyshire* (1860, 1870 edns)

Higgins, A., 'A Hand to Mouth Existence': Women's Lives in Holmewood before 1950 (Derbyshire County Council, *c*.1993)

*Kelly's Directory of Derbyshire* (1895, 1899 edns)

Kettle, P., *The* Hardwick Inn (1991)

Kettle, P., *Oldcotes. The Last Mansion built by Bess of Hardwick* (Cardiff, 2000)

Lees-Milne, J., *The Bachelor Duke. William Spencer Cavendish 6th Duke of Devonshire 1790-1858* (1991)

Lysons, D. and S., *Magna Britannia. V. Derbyshire* (London, 1817)

Markham, V., *Paxton and the Bachelor Duke* (London, 1935)

National Trust, *A Short Guide to Hardwick Park* (n.d.)

Pearson, J., *The Serpent and the Stag* (New York, 1983)

Pevsner, N. and Williamson, E., *The Buildings of England. Derbyshire* (London, 1979)

Pilkington, J., *A View of the Present State of Derbyshire* (London, 1789)

Riden, P., *Tudor and Stuart Chesterfield* (Chesterfield, 1984)

Riden, P. (ed.), *George Sitwell's Letterbook 1662-66* (Derbyshire Record Society, 10, 1985)

Riden, P., 'The charcoal iron industry in the East Midlands 1580-1780', *DAJ*, 111 (1991), 64-84

Riden, P. (ed.), *Derbyshire Directories 1781-1824* (Derbyshire Record Society, 33, 2006)

Riden, P., 'Bess of Hardwick and the St Loe inheritance' in Riden, P. and Edwards, D.G. (eds), *Essays in Derbyshire History presented to Gladwyn Turbutt* (Derbyshire Record Society, 30, 2006), 80-106.

Riden, P., 'Sir William Cavendish: Tudor civil servant and founder of a dynasty', *DAJ*, 129 (2009), 238-57

Riden, P., 'The Hardwicks of Hardwick Hall in the fifteenth and sixteenth centuries', *DAJ*, 130 (2010)

Riden, P. and Fowkes, D., *Bolsover: Castle, Town and Colliery* (2008)

Riden, P. and Gordon, R. (eds), *Derbyshire Population Statistics 1563-2001* (Derbyshire Record Society, forthcoming)

Sheppard, R., 'The Evidence for Changes to Farm Buildings on the Devonshire Estate in the Parish of Ault Hucknall, Derbyshire, during the mid-late 19th century' (Unpublished report by Trent & Peak Archaeology, 2008; copies in Chesterfield and Matlock local studies libraries)

Thompson, F., *A History of Chatsworth* (London, 1949)

Tinniswood, A., *The Verneys* (New York, 2007)

Tranter, E.M. (ed.), *The Derbyshire Returns to the 1851 Religious Census* (Derbyshire Record Society, 23, 1995)

Turberville, A.S., *A History of Welbeck Abbey and its Owners* (London, 1938)

Turbutt, G., *A History of Ogston* (Ogston, 1975)

Turner, P., *A Social History of the Village of Holmewood 1868-1968* (Derbyshire, 1980)

Walters, J.T., *The Building of Twelve Thousand Houses* (London, 1927)

Warrener, T., *A History of Nether Langwith, Langwith & Whaley Thorns* (1999)

*White's Directory of Derbyshire* (1857)

*White's Directory of Sheffield* (1852, 1862 edns)

Willies, L., 'The Barker family and the eighteenth-century lead business', *DAJ*, 93 (1973), 55-74

Worsley, L., *Hardwick Old Hall* (Swindon, 1998)

Wragg, B. and Worsley, G. (eds), *The Life and Works of John Carr of York* (York, 2000)

## SUGGESTIONS FOR FUTHER READING

There is a large general literature on most of the topics on which this book touches, apart from the local and specialised works cited in the endnotes and listed in the bibliography. Readers who would like to pursue the subject further may find the following of interest. As well as general books, the list includes some family and local material not included in the endnotes.

Airs, M., *The Making of the English Country House* (1975)

Beard, M., *English Landed Society in the Twentieth Century* (1989)

Beckett, J.V., *The Aristocracy in England 1660-1914* (1986)

Beckett, J.V., *The East Midlands from AD 1000* (1988)

Bernard, G.W., *The Power of the Early Tudor Nobility. A Study of the Fourth and Fifth Earls of Shrewsbury* (1985)

Cannadine, D., *Lords and Landlords: the Aristocracy and the Towns 1774-1967* (1980)

Clemenson, H., *English Country Houses and Landed Estates* (1982)

Cliffe, J.T., *The World of the Country House in Seventeenth-Century England* (1999)

Dawson, M., *Plenti and Grase. Food and Drink in a Sixteenth-Century Household* (2009)

Devonshire, Deborah Dowager Duchess of, *The House. A Portrait of Chatsworth* (1982)

Friedman, A.T., *House and Household in Elizabethan England. Wollaton Hall and the Willoughby Family* (1989)

Girouard, M., *Life in the English Country House. A Social and Architectural History* (1978)

Girouard, M., *The Victorian Country House* (1979)

Guinness, J. and C., *The House of Mitford* (1984)

Hainsworth, D.R., *Stewards, Lords and People. The Estate Steward and his World in Later Stuart England* (1992)

Heale, F. and Holmes, C., *The Gentry in England and Wales, 1500-1700* (1994)

Heape, R.G., *Buxton under the Dukes of Devonshire* (1948)

Hey, D., *Packmen, Carriers and Packhorse Roads. Trade and Communications in North Derbyshire and South Yorkshire* (1980)

Hey, D., *Derbyshire. A History* (2008)

Levey, S.M., *Elizabethan Treasures. The Hardwick Hall Textiles* (1998)

Masters, B., *The Dukes. The Origins, Ennoblement and History of Twenty-six Families* (1975)

Mingay, G.E., *English Landed Society in the Eighteenth Century* (1963)

Perrott, R., *The Aristocrats. A Portrait of Britain's Nobility and their Way of Life Today* (1968)

Stone, L., *The Crisis of the Aristocracy 1558-1641* (1965)

Stone, L., *Family and Fortune. Studies in Aristocratic Finance in the Sixteenth and Seventeenth Centuries* (1973)

Stone, L. and J.C.F., *An Open Elite? England 1540-1880* (1984)

Thompson, F.M.L., *English Landed Society in the Nineteenth Century* (1963)

Thompson, G.S., *Life in a Noble Household 1641-1700* (1965)

Wilson, R. and Mackley, A., *Creating Paradise. The Building of the English Country House 1660-1880* (2000)

# Index

Places are in general indexed under civil parishes; except where indicated, all parishes are in Derbyshire. Peers are indexed under family names, women, as far as possible, under maiden names.

## Picture Credits

The authors and publishers wish to thank the following for permission to reproduce their material. Any infringement of copyright is entirely accidental: every care has been taken to contact or trace all copyright owners. We would be pleased to correct in future editions any errors or omissions brought to our attention. References are to page numbers except where stated.

Chesterfield Borough Council, 55
City of London (Guildhall Library and Guildhall Art Gallery), 42 (Fig. 32), 53
City of London (London Metropolitan Archives), 75
David Templeman, 24
Derbyshire Archaeological Society, 85 (Fig. 53)
Derbyshire Library Service, 96, 97
Devonshire Collection, Chatsworth. Reproduced by permission of Chatsworth Settlement Trustees, 15 (Fig. 14), 16, 57, 70, 90, 108, 121
English Heritage (Steve Cole) 47, 58, 68, 85 (Fig. 52), 94, 95 (Fig. C), 112, 113, 115, 130, 134, 136 (Fig. 84), 138, 139, 142, 159, 169; (Photo Library), 30, 34, 46 (Fig. A), 103, 141
English Heritage (NMR © Crown Copyright), 18 (Fig. 17), 27 (Fig. B), 152
F. Fowkes, 117
Giraffe/Derby Cathedral, 36
Images of England (Dr Eric Ritchie), 87, 106; (with permission of National Trust), 123
Mary Evans Picture Library, 53
National Trust Picture Library, 31, 150; (David Levenson), 8; (John Bethell), 10; (Hawkley Studios), 21; (Derek Croucher), 27 (Fig. D); (Andreas von Einsiedel), 29; (Nadia Mackenzie), 35
Ordnance Survey, 127, 129, 133, 157
Picture the Past www.picturethepast.org.uk, 1, 6, 23, 61, 73, 78, 89, 99, 104, 125, 128, 131, 135, 140, 154, 158 (Courtesy of *Derbyshire Times*), 160, 161, 165, 166, 174; (Courtesy of *Mansfield Chad*), 111; (Courtesy of Mrs G.M. Ravey), 119
Private Collection, 2
Survey of London, 45
Pictures of England/Jez Taylor, 19
RIBA Library Photographs Collection, 33
Staveley Neighbourhood Management, 63
Thoroton Society of Nottinghamshire, 27 (Fig. C)
Trent and Peak Archaeology, 115, 116
University of London, x, 14, 15, 18, 28, 32, 42, 46 (Fig. B), 74, 80, 82, 83, 95 (Fig. B), 110, 137, 148, 151, 162, 168, 173, 175
www.webaviation.co.uk, 5

The following maps were drawn by Cath D'Alton, Figs 4, 8, 11, 30, 35, 41, Panel 1 – Fig. A. © University of London.